A Boy's Seasons

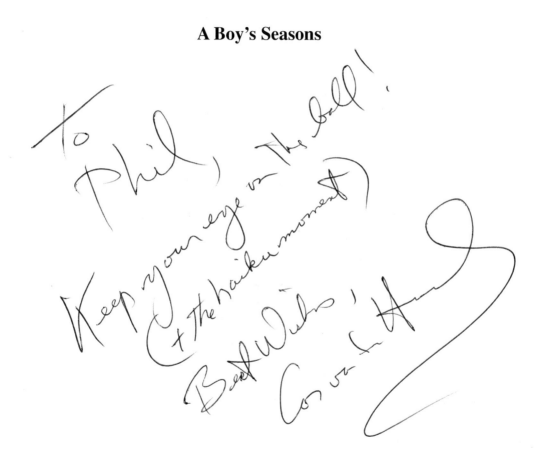

To Phil,

Keep your eye on the ball!
(t the haiku moment)

Best Wishes,
Cor Van Hus

Other Works by Cor van den Heuvel

sun in skull [Haiku], Chant Press, New York City, 1961.
a bag of marbles (3 jazz chants), Chant Press, 1962.
the window-washer's pail [Haiku], Chant Press, 1963.
EO7 [Haiku Sequence], Chant Press, 1964.
BANG! you're dead. [Poem], Chant Press, 1966.
water in a stone depression [Haiku], Chant Press, 1969.
dark [Haiku], Chant Press, 1982.
PUDDLES [Haibun], Chant Press, 1990.
The Geese Have Gone [Haiku], King's Road Press, Pointe Claire, Quebec, 1992.
Play Ball [Baseball Haiku], Red Moon Press, Winchester, Virginia, 1999.

As Editor:
The Haiku Anthology, Doubleday Anchor, New York City, 1974; Simon &
Schuster, New York City, 1986; W. W. Norton, New York City, 1999.
The Haiku Path, (Co-Editor with various others), The Haiku Society of
America, New York City, 1994.
Wedge of Light [Haibun], (Co-Editor with Tom Lynch and Michael Dylan
Welch), Press Here, Foster City, California, 1999.
Past Time [Baseball Haiku], (Co-Editor with Jim Kacian), Red Moon Press,
Winchester, Virginia, 1999.
Baseball Haiku, (Co-Editor with Nanae Tamura), W. W. Norton, New York City, 2007.

A Boy's Seasons

haibun memoirs

Cor van den Heuvel

Single Island Press
2010

Acknowledgments: "A Boy's Seasons" and "A Boy's Holidays" first appeared
in *Modern Haiku* (1993, 1995). "The Paper Route" first appeared in
The Persimmon Tree (1990). There have been a number of changes in these works
since they were published in those magazines. Portions of the "Dixie Lid Cowboys"
haibun originally appeared, in a different form, in *Argosy* magazine (1974).

ISBN: 978-0-9740895-8-4
Published by Single Island Press
379 State Street, Portsmouth, N.H. 03801, U.S.A.

Cover design by Susan Kress Hamilton
Cover photograph courtesy of Shirley Hodgdon

Printed in the United States of America

To my
Mother and Father

Lily Yuill and Dirk Jan van den Heuvel

Some Special Thank Yous

I would like to thank the following members of The Spring Street Haiku Group for listening to early drafts of *A Boy's Seasons* and giving me invaluable criticism and advice: Carl Patrick, Karen Sohne, Evan Mahl, and Doris Heitmeyer. Carl Patrick's suggestions were particularly useful to me. He and Karen Sohne also aided me in the editing of "A Boy's Holidays" and "Fights." Karen Sohne pointed out ways to improve some of the haiku in "The Paper Route" and suggested the "pots and pans" finale in the "reading the western" sequence in "Christmas." These discussions were not only helpful to me in doing the final revisions, but gave me relief from the solitary work of writing. After each of the sessions, which were held in my Greenwich Village (East) apartment, we went to a nearby restaurant for food and drink and more talk.

The Spring Street Haiku Group met monthly for about ten years at Poets House, when it was on Spring Street (in Manhattan), to read and discuss works in progress. Organized in 1992 by Dee Evetts, it brings together ten or so members of The Haiku Society of America in a more intensive workshop atmosphere than is practicable at the Society's meetings.

And a special thanks to my wife, Leigh Larrecq van den Heuvel, for her advice and encouragement—and for helping to make the dreams of the boy in this book come true.

CONTENTS

The Kaleidoscopic Year:
A Preface in the Form of a Letter to the Author

There is so much to admire in *A Boy's Seasons*: the mysterious power of individual haiku; the way the haiku seem to condense out of their context and drop onto the page, giving new resilience to the haibun form; the pure American wine poured into old sake bottles; the humor; the intensity of a boy's perceptions coupled with that double perspective of nostalgia that saturates our memory. . . .

The "swish of the net" haiku is a finale any circus would envy and, more important, it is the verbal equivalent of a boy's perfect hookshot—a haiku shot—and it is the hookshot hinted at in the introductory haibun, "The Seasons." Your piece begins and ends with the same image, as the seasons come full circle. And the boy's practice shots have borne the fruit of the poet's perfection.

As I understand it, the title refers to two different structural principles: the four seasons and the seasons of a boy's developing life, marked by his preoccupations. Hearing the title, one might think of psychological stages before one thinks of spring through winter. And one might think those stages of growing up would proceed chronologically: marbles and Dixie cups, cowboys and Indians first, then baseball and so on as motor skills mature. But no. You have suspended the activities of childhood in a kind of time warp, an eternal present, a perpetual nostalgia machine, by placing these activities in the context of the year cycle.

This is fitting, because childhood seems a timeless period, an endless moment, insulated from the deadlines and entropy of the adult's world. As the seasons unfold, a boy's connection to them unfolds regardless of the boy's age; the bundled-up kid tumbling in the snow and the high school senior practicing hookshots in the gym inhabit the same season. It's just a boy and winter, followed by a boy and spring. As the kaleidoscopic year turns, the pattern shifts, and it is always the present, where the haiku poet breathes and has his being.

Carl Patrick

Introduction

A Boy's Seasons:
Baseball, Football, and Basketball

This book is about a boy growing up in mid-20th Century America. Like many other boys of his generation the seasons for him were defined by the sports he played and loved. By the time he was into his teens, spring and summer had become baseball season, fall was football season, and winter was basketball season. Along with these major sports, other interests pursued by boys of this period are affectionately evoked in these pages. Some came earlier in this boy's life, such as marbles, hideouts, and skating. Some were enjoyed through all of his boyhood like going to the beach and to amusement parks. His participation in, and his feelings about, our traditional holidays are carefully delineated and called to life in a long section called "A Boy's Holidays."

More than just a memoir in the form of personal essays, this book is in a new form in English that has become very popular on websites and literary magazines devoted to haiku and its related genres: it's called haibun, a mixed form of prose and haiku. It's an ideal form for this star-spangled red-white-and-blue book. We experience with the boy what he feels when he watches the flag go by in the Memorial Day parade, for we see the parade through his haiku-like awareness. Haiku moments involve the senses: seeing, hearing, smelling, tasting, or touching. You don't have to be a haiku poet to have such moments. Any of us can have one if we see or hear something so vividly and clearly that we have a feeling of unity, or oneness, with *it*, and by extension with Nature itself. It may be something as simple as the sound of your dog lapping water from his bowl in the kitchen on a hot summer day or the sight of spring sunlight shining on some sheets blowing on the line. For the boy in this book it may be the coolness of his glove as he plays centerfield in the late afternoon shadows of a ballpark or the lonely sound of his basketball bouncing on the floor of an empty gym on a rainy, winter day.

Many moments in the book are about such simple, ordinary things. But others are atypical: such as the blow-by-blow descriptions of several important fights the boy has, one cheered on by a WWII troop train stopped at a railroad crossing; and the reliving of the time he goes to the circus and falls in love with the beautiful bareback rider. He also experiences the confusions of adolescence. When he walks his paper route along a snowy country road, he thinks longingly about the pretty girl having supper in the next house, yet becomes tongue-tied and awkward in her presence. When he feels a teenager's skepticism about Easter or Christmas, or finds himself getting into a fight, he feels uncertain about what life is all about. But, when he stands waiting at the plate and a summer breeze comes across the field, or he is running through the slanting light of autumn to catch a touchdown pass, such troubled thoughts are far away. He is alive and happy in the moment.

Cor van den Heuvel
New York City, November 2009

A Boy's Seasons

The Seasons

At first there were just two seasons: winter and summer. There was cold and there was heat. The sign for winter was snow, for summer the sun. In winter my mother bundled me up and I went out to tumble in the snow or to go sledding. Maine back in the 'thirties had winters with whirling, blinding blizzards, snowdrifts piling up five and six feet high, frosted windows, rows of icicles hanging from roofs, clanking tire chains, and plows throwing great waves of snow to the sides of the road. Sometimes a record snowfall temporarily froze and muffled our world and we woke up to a hushed landscape of deep drifts and snow-weighted trees. My shouts seemed to dwindle away in this cold white stillness, but I left my mark on it by rolling the snow up into a great ball.

In summer it was hot. I wore shorts and played in the sun, which was no longer away off on a distant horizon but right overhead. I played out on the lawn or in the grassy fields, or at the beach. We lived a short drive from the ocean, and went there often. And if we couldn't get to the ocean, there was the river, or the lake, or the sprinkler on the lawn. Summer was sunlight and water and I would spend hours playing in the waves of the sea or in the shallows of a pond.

As I got older, I began to separate spring and autumn from the flow of the year. At first, one was simply the promise of summer, the other the forerunner, or warning, of winter. Then I became aware of things that made them different: the flowers and birds of spring, the slanting light and falling leaves of autumn.

When we moved to New Hampshire in the fall of 1940, our new home was only thirty-seven miles from where we'd lived in Maine, so the seasons were still the same. But the way I saw the seasons continued to change. I was now in the fourth grade and almost ten years old. Well, nine-and-a-half. As I grew into my teens, the seasons of New England began to take on more and more distinct shapes—not just from a change of cold to hot, or from such things as spring blossoms and autumn leaves, but from baseball, football, and basketball. Drawn to each of these sports at different times of the year, I devoted all my time and energy to them, practicing over and over again the way to swing a bat, kick a football, or make a jump shot. And playing every chance I got.

This devotion was a kind of religion. With my mind and body totally involved in the practice or playing of these sports I felt a oneness with my surroundings, and by extension with the universe. The mind became clear. Set only in the direction of completing an act of beauty and grace—though never thought of in such sissy terms, but rather as a feat of strength and skill—it, the mind, became completely united with my body and together they moved through space and time to a pitch of motion that sometimes passed into the wonder of perfection, the perfect swing, the perfect pass into the end zone, or the perfect hookshot floating up in a flowing arc to fall with a whisper through the strings of the basket.

first warm day
fitting my fingers into the mitt
pounding the pocket

When it was warm and sunny enough for us to get out a ball and gloves for a game of catch, we knew winter was over. A baseball flying through the air was our sign of spring. We loved the sight of it the way a Japanese haiku poet loves to see the first plum blossom flowering in a still snowy landscape. A baseball was our plum blossom. Blossoming in the blue skies of early spring when snow and puddles still lingered along the side of the road, it would continue to bloom all summer long.

summer afternoon
the long fly ball to center field
takes its time

When the leaves began to turn color and started falling, and there was a frostiness in the air, it was time to switch to throwing and kicking a football.

chill wind
a football twirls through
the falling leaves

When the ground got hard and snow began to fall it was time to play basketball, hopefully in a gym, but if not, we shoveled out the snow around the basket in the backyard.

winter rain
the sound of the basketball
in the empty gym

So for me there were three main seasons: baseball, football, and basketball. And the four natural seasons became their backdrop.

Along with these sports, my life as a boy included many other activities that kept me outdoors and made me aware of nature's round of the seasons. In the spring I sailed popsicle-stick boats in gutter streams, played marbles, flipped bubble-gum cards, flew kites, and went fishing. Summer was swimming, bicycling, cutting the grass, going to amusement parks, and lying under a tree reading comic books. Autumn was county fairs, "hunting" with my dog, playing kick-the-can, raking leaves, and running long-distance. Winter had hockey, skiing, sledding, shoveling the driveway, and snowball fights. Many of these were played around the house: in the yard or in the neighboring fields and woods. Some indoor activities, such as reading books, listening to the radio, and going to the movies, were pursued all year, but more often in the winter because of its bad weather and shorter days. As I got deeper into my teens, I began to concentrate more on the three major sports, and either gave up many of my other games and activities—indoor and outdoor—or spent less time on them.

My favorite pastime in the years before my life became sports was playing I was someone else—a cowboy or an Indian, a superhero or a soldier. I would adapt these games of "pretending" to the seasonal circumstances. In winter, with my dog hitched to my sled, I became a Royal Mountie crossing the frozen Yukon. In the summer, a sandy beach might set the scene for a ride through the desert as The Lone Ranger—"Hi-Yo Silver, Away!"

When I later turned to sports it was to be myself, to perfect myself, to become a great athlete. I set up schedules: so much time for lifting weights in the garage, so much for running cross-country on old lumber roads in the nearby woods, so much for throwing baskets at the hoop in the backyard. Though I never came close to being a great athlete, the experience of going through the rituals of exercise, practice, and playing was in itself reward enough for the time and sweat I offered up to these games, especially since over the years it included having my share of those magical moments when everything clicks into place and time seems to stop to take note of it, though no one else might.

As a boy I didn't recognize the importance of the natural world around me. I did belong to the Boy Scouts a while and even went to summer camp. I remember the smell of fly dope and washing up in the cold lake at sunrise. We climbed a mountain, sang "bump on a log," were homesick, had bonfires, flag-raising ceremonies, and swimming lessons. I made a beaded belt, tied knots, learned to spot the Pleiades, and generally got acquainted with living in the woods. So, I had contact with nature, but from a practical how-to-chop-firewood and paddle-a-canoe approach. I reached First-Class in the Scouts and then lost interest in collecting more merit badges—I'd rather collect base hits.

The books I liked to read were mostly boys' adventure novels about cowboys and Indians. Every Christmas there was a new Lone Ranger book under the tree with the Lone Ranger and Tonto galloping their horses out of the bright glossy colors of the bookjacket. I also liked books about dogs and always had a dog when I was a kid. Reading cowboy books and dog stories brought nature into the world of my imagination, but didn't make me particularly attentive to the nature around me—especially since the cowboy books were about western landscapes.

The seasons as expressions of a spirit in nature (and my own being) was not something I was aware of until I went to college and began to read Keats and Hopkins, Emerson and Thoreau, and started hiking and backpacking into the woods and mountains by myself. Later I discovered the Japanese haiku poets and learned how even the simplest things in the natural world related to me. Haiku showed me I was a part of nature and the flow of the seasons. When I was a boy I was also a part of that flow but I was not conscious of it. I might feel an animal pleasure in the spring sunlight as I took part in a game of catch, but I didn't think of it as "nature"—it simply made the day a great day for playing baseball.

spring rain
waiting on the front porch
with my ball and glove

Spring

Spring is mud . . . and baseball. Warm sunlight and warm breezes mingling with a coolness from the still cold earth and the melting snows of winter. It's a white ball flying through the air, from one leather glove to another—back and forth—until, missing one of the gloves, it lands on the spongy lawn among patches of dirty snow—or splashes into a mud puddle in the driveway. Spring's an open window in the classroom and a strange restlessness in the class. Sweaters tied around the neck or waist. The softness and glitter of girls coming out from under coats and hats and fluttering in the sunny breezes. It's your dog running through puddles and chasing nothing at all back and forth across the front lawn. It's standing in the outfield waiting for the ball to come your way while the cries float out from the infield: "Atta boy, Lefty . . . No hitter up there." It's marbles and bubble-gum cards and pussy willows. It's riding your bike off ramps made with boards on heaped-up dirt and flying through the air with a sinking feeling in your stomach. It's swinging like Tarzan from limb to limb through the trees budding with new leaves. It's hanging out on street corners, dreaming in the library, running on a baseball field, going fishing in the pond, getting tongue-tied in front of a pretty girl. It's a feeling of loosening bonds, rising energy, wild abandon—freedom. And baseball.

baseball cards
spread out on the bed
April rain

even the baseball is chilly —
wearing a warm-up jacket
while warming up

geese flying north
the pitcher stops his windup
to watch

spring practice
his curve ball curves more
in the growing darkness

a game of catch
the dog turns his head
back and forth

through the blue sky
the tape-wrapped baseball trails
a black streamer

under the lights
hitting it out of the park
and into the night

1. Marbles and Bubble-Gum Cards

Before baseball replaced them in the fifth or sixth grade, marbles were linked most closely in my mind with the mud of spring. These brilliant and glittering glass spheres were brought out after most of the snow had melted, flowering out of pockets, boxes, and bags into the spring sunshine. We looked around the puddle and mud-pocked schoolyard at recess to find some dry ground to play on. We didn't play "regular" marbles: shooting them out of a circle. Maybe all that spring mud we get in northern New England discouraged us from getting down on our hands and knees.

We had a game where two boys stood several feet apart with a marble on the ground between them. Each took turns trying to hit it with another marble. You didn't flip the "shooter" with the back of your thumb, but held it between the ends of thumb and forefinger and threw or tossed it from about chest level. If you hit the one on the ground you won a marble, or more, from the other kid.

> the toy sailboat
> sails across the puddle
> with a cargo of two marbles

Another popular game was with marbles and a cigarbox. Boys brought cigarboxes to school with a small circular hole cut in the cover. If you could drop a marble through the hole, dropping it from waist high into the box on the ground, the owner of the box had to give you several of his marbles plus the one you had dropped. He got all those that missed. The hole was barely big enough to let the average-sized marble go in. You had to make a direct hit.

When the box was picked up you could hear the marbles inside rolling and clicking together. In the bag of marbles you sometimes carried with you, the marbles also made clicking sounds, but cleaner and less harsh than those that came from the box. In the soft cloth bag, there was a nice contrast between the hardness of each marble, signaled by the clicks, and the liquid flow of all the marbles when you changed the bag's shape by handling it. Reaching into the bag, you could also roll the marbles through your fingers and feel the cool, smooth, contained curves of glass. The clicking had a sharp, precise sound that seemed like the broken fragments of an icy, mathematical music. It confirmed the clear solidity, the purity, of the material world, yet called up like an Indian's ceremonial rattle a kind of magic within or beyond it.

Depending on the boy, or his mood, the games and the trading that went on had either the goal of collecting a lot of marbles or getting what he thought were the most beautiful ones—or both. I think marbles (and girls and cars when you got older) were the only things a boy would use the word "beauty" for: "That's a beauty," or "beaut" for short. You'd need a lot of so-so marbles to play with and to swap for the prized beauties, which were sometimes too big to go through the hole in the box anyway.

a spinning top
moves along the sidewalk
towards the girls' jacks

There were many kinds of marbles. There were the sparkling glassies that you could see right through. Some of these were like little crystal balls, so clear and pure you could imagine little visions floating through them. Others had a slight color tint like a pale blue sky or a pale rose glow. Still others would have ribbons of color floating down in the depths of them or twisting through the clear part. Sometimes there seemed to be a frosting of tiny bubbles scattered through the tinted crystal like you see in some glass paperweights. Then there were the solid-color marbles that could have every color of the rainbow or any one or any combination. In swirls or bars or twirling dots, in speckles or stripes, and in colors soft and pale or deep and bold. Some of the colors would glow or glitter. They might seem sprinkled with gold dust or flakes of blue or red jewels.

Sometimes you'd find a marble so unique that when you got it, you said to yourself, now I'll give up this crazy game and just keep this. But then you'd see another one.

> the crystal marble
> on the bedside table
> full moon

Bubble-gum cards were traded and gambled for like the marbles and I associated them with the sunny days of spring, too. But the game you played with the cards involved flipping them towards and against the schoolyard's board fence. Since they landed on the ground, you didn't want to play anywhere near any puddles or mud. As in pitching pennies, the player whose card came closest to the fence won all the cards thrown. A card that fluttered down to end up leaning against the fence was a sure winner—unless a later toss knocked it away.

There were all sorts of cards: baseball players, animals, soldiers, famous cowboys, frontiersmen, warships, airplanes, and Indians. Except for some treasured favorites, they all flew through the air and landed on the earth in front of the fence. I liked the portraits of famous Indian Chiefs best. There was something about the nobility of the feather-bedecked figure against a background showing a forest wilderness, or the mountains, or the plains, along with the sense that the card was a window onto a way of life lost forever, yet right here in my hand, printed in mint-fresh glittering colors, on stiff and permanent cardboard, that made these pieces of ephemera glow with the immediate and almost tangible presence of the old West.

spring day
an Indian Chief bubble-gum card
by the schoolyard fence

2. Baseball Season

Spring was baseball. The first sunlit breezes of March drew me to my mitt, which had lain all winter on a bookshelf in my bedroom, well oiled and tied tightly around a baseball lodged in its pocket. The sunlight and breezes—a mix of cool and warm air—sparkling and flowing among puddles, trees, and grasses, around patches of leftover snow, and along the wet sides of roads, made me want to play a game of catch, to swing my arm through the slow and easy, then gradually faster and harder, motions of throwing a baseball: to send the ball sailing through the air so it smacks firmly into someone else's glove, then see it whirling back towards me and feel and hear it land with a solid, socking sound into my own mitt.

> March thaw
> the sounds of a game of catch
> from the driveway

Something so simple—just the throwing of that round, hard ball back and forth, over and over again. It seemed as if it could go on forever in the warm sunlight of spring afternoons. Sometimes in the loose grip of that repeated motion, fantasies of games and triumphs to come later in the season might rise up against the backdrop of the clear blue sky, and I would feel my arm bearing down even harder to send the ball whistling into the distant glove. (Look at that curveball! Maybe I should be a pitcher.) But most of the time it was only a mindless repetition—the ball just going back and forth—thought was simply turned off. My body and my "self" disappeared into the pleasure of the continuing moment. There was a timelessness about it. Everything resolved into the joy of the movement, the motion that didn't go anywhere.

> the ball sky-high
> as the crack of the bat
> reaches the outfield

Later, as the areas of dry ground increased in size and the last of the snow hid deep under hedges or behind the garage, out would come the bat and the solid sound of ash against horsehide would be added to our song of spring. Then would come the pickup games in a field almost surrounded by the still-cool woods—and once in a while I would swing away in just the right smooth pulling motion and the bat would send the ball soaring high and far, flying way over the pine trees beyond left field.

a spring breeze
flutters the notice
for baseball tryouts

Baseball season would continue on into the long days of summer, too, and there would even be warm, or hot, afternoons when we'd get to play on a regulation diamond in the park and do the long, slow dance of a "real" baseball game—punctuated with the regular swift movements from the mound to the plate and the sudden flurries of action around the bases or in the outfield—on into evening and right into dusk, until we could no longer see the ball and I'd walk home under the newly risen moon to a cold supper, which my mother would reheat for me.

at the plate
looking out from under my cap
at the world

the batter checks
the placement of his feet
"Strike One!"

the infield chatter
floats out to deep center
summer breeze

slow inning
the right fielder is playing
with a dog

light rain
the line drive knocks up dust
from the wet basepath

changing pitchers
the runner on first looks up
at a passing cloud

picking up my glove
from the shade in right field
its coolness

after the game
a full moon rises over
the left-field fence

3. Dixie Lid Cowboys

A hot day sometime in the 'forties in Dover, New Hampshire. After finishing a pickup game of baseball in the park, I stop for some ice cream at a small drugstore on the way home. Stepping out of the store, the screen-door swinging shut behind me, I carry a Dixie cup of ice cream in one hand, a flat wooden spoon in the other, and my baseball glove under one arm.

Still sweating from the game (the drugstore has only a lazy overhead fan) I stand in the dark shade of the drugstore awning and look for a second at the heat waves bouncing up and down in the street. Then trying to balance everything, I slowly take the circular cardboard lid off the cup, and peer at it closely as I slowly turn it over, looking through the film of ice cream sticking to its underside, hoping to catch sight of a ten-gallon hat in the picture hidden there. A quick lick with my tongue takes away the coating of half-chocolate, half-vanilla ice cream and I can see through the wax paper that covers the black and white photograph that it *is* of a cowboy, and it looks like . . . it *is* Buck Jones.

in the dent
of his ten-gallon hat
a faint shadow

The Dixie lid movie series included 24 different stars every year—from glamorous beauty queens to famous comedians—and only four or five were cowboys, so it was rare to get a western star and rarer to get one of my favorites like Buck Jones or Hopalong Cassidy. You could trade 24 lids for an 8 inch by 10 inch hand-colored photograph of any star in the series. On the back of this would be several black and white photographs of scenes from that star's latest movie.

> the wonder horse, Tony, rears up
> in the Tom Mix autographed picture
> —Tom waves his hat

Sticking the wooden spoon into the cup of ice cream, I continue my balancing act so I can peel the paper off the picture on the lid. I pull it free slowly, because it sticks to the wax that coats the surface of the cardboard photograph, and also to enjoy—like a poker player slowly fanning his cards—the gradual appearance of the crystal-clear image of the cowboy. Moving to the edge of the awning I hold it closer to the sunlight. Now completely revealed, the picture glistens "wet" and alive in its glossy coat of wax.

Through this round porthole I look into another world. If I could only see over the lower edge, I'd see his white horse, and the sagebrush . . . and somewhere beyond his ten-gallon hat must be the prairie and the distant mountains. The lids always showed only the star's head, or his head and shoulders, but my imagination could get the cowboy to rear his horse right out of the surface of the cardboard.

Only after I've satisfied my imagination this way do I turn my attention to what is in the cup. By this time the ice cream is getting soft. I *like* soft ice cream.

Years later, I would occasionally notice the round cardboard cover from an ice cream cup lying on a sidewalk with its top side up (the side printed with the ice cream manufacturer's name) and would nostalgically kick it over, half-hoping to see, as it rolled into the gutter and turned over, Buck Jones staring steely-eyed up at me from under the brim of his white ten-gallon hat. But I never did. And after a while there were no pictures of any kind under Dixie lids, only blank spaces.

in the bookcase
a cowboy Dixie lid
leans on a baseball

Summer

Summer is heat . . . and more baseball. Long days of baseball in the hot sun, playing on an old meadow with an occasional pine-scented breeze coming out of the woods, or on a regulation diamond with a real mound and with mowed grass in the outfield. It's pounding the pocket of your catcher's mitt and feeling the dirt under your feet behind home plate. Summer is hitching a ride to a lake or the seaside with a rolled towel under your arm, working at summer jobs, daring each other to walk across a girder on a railroad trestle or to dive into the pond from a high branch. It's lazing on the porch with a comic book. Riding a bike to feel the cool rush of air on your face. It's the glare of chrome from cars. Steam rising from a glittering pavement when the sun comes out after a sudden downpour. All the cows under the one tree in the meadow. A cicada sounding like electricity buzzing through the telephone poles. Your dog's tongue hanging out. It's the smell of cut grass. The lawn under your bare feet. A cowboy hideout under the cool pines. It's going to amusement parks and carnivals, riding the roller coaster and the merry-go-round, playing a game of ring-toss and winning a penny whistle instead of the pair of binoculars. Hamburgers and milkshakes. It's girls in summer dresses

walking along the sunny sidewalks or in bathing suits lying by the sea. The fresh tight feel of your skin and the coiled energy of your whole body after a long day at the beach when you take a shower and pull on a cool, clean shirt. It's sitting at the supper table eating your fifth ear of corn while the evening sun is still coming through the open back door. It's thinking of the girl you sat next to in class and whom you haven't seen all summer when you are sitting alone on the front porch and the moon rises.

And it's once going all the way to Boston with your father for a Red Sox game and coming out into the stands of Fenway Park to see all that breeze-blown sparkling green grass under an endless panoramic blue pennant-waving sky. Then from a seat right behind first base you watch Ted Williams, Dom DiMaggio, Bobby Doerr and Johnny Pesky, and all the rest of "the greatest team never to win a World Series" run from the dugout to take the field, and you see and hear the umpire yell through the roar of the crowd the time-honored words: "Play ball!"

Ted hits another homer
a seagull high over right field
gets out of the way

hot day
listening to the ballgame
while washing the car

summer afternoon
the coolness of the newspaper
from the grocery bag

after a loop over the lawn
the balsa-wood glider glides
behind enemy lines

late breeze
shucking corn for supper
on the back porch

the open backdoor
evening sunlight shines
in the dog's waterdish

cooling on the steps
the sunset colors the sky
and our T-shirts

while doing the dishes
my mother sings
Roamin' in the Gloamin'

summer night
playing on the kitchen floor
the cool linoleum

moths fly around
the roadside ice cream stand
moon above the pines

1. The Beach

I was born, and lived the first years of my life, by the banks of the Saco River, near where it enters the sea in southern Maine. I have always felt a closeness to water, especially the ocean, and have rarely lived far from it.

"Going to the beach," which I did quite often as a boy, was not a sport, though it could have been the setting for the pursuit of a number of them. It was just play, even as I grew into my teens. There was no challenge to excel like I felt with baseball or basketball. I didn't try to become a great swimmer; the ocean in Maine was usually too cold to swim in for very long anyway. I just enjoyed riding the waves—body surfing—and diving into the blue-green immensity of the Atlantic Ocean. Or I would take long walks along the shoreline, finding skate's eggs, crabs and jellyfish—and hoping to find pieces-of-eight from a pirate's buried treasure.

When I was only two- or three-feet high I had a tin pail and shovel with which I created imaginary worlds out of sand and water. I would get tanned and elastic in the hot sun—and have dreams of faraway places that took shape along the ocean's horizon or in the turrets of sand castles.

a breeze at sunset
the toy sailboat sails slowly
around the pail

As twilight spreads along the beach my mother comes across the wet sands of the retreating tide and tells me, after I've been playing there all afternoon, to get out of the cold water—"Your lips have turned blue." I free myself from the dancing waves and dreams of sailing ships and desert islands and reluctantly trudge up the beach. Suddenly I'm very hungry and I start running, dreaming now of hot dogs and sodas. Or some french fries from one of the stands on the pier.

cool salt air
the merry-go-round whirls
in the candied apples

Back in the 'thirties and early 'forties, the amusement pier at Old Orchard Beach, Maine, had one of the biggest, most beautiful merry-go-rounds in the world. In 1940, when I was nine, we moved there for several months. We'd always lived in the general area and had gone down to the beach fairly often in the summer—by automobile or on the open-air trolley car—but now I could just walk down the street from our house and be at the edge of the ocean, below the roller coaster, or out on the pier.

When we moved, I had a big black part-Newfoundland dog, Buster, who used to go with me everywhere. We hardly ever had any money so he and I used to sneak rides on the merry-go-round. I would always head for my favorite: a prancing white horse with a blue saddle. The swirls of wood in the horse's mane and in the sweep of its tail were magical details that reflected the flowing contours of that hoofed wonder's whole body.

All the horses were wonderful: the way they would swing around in the curved path of the carousel platform, some of them moving up and down while whirling around, others just whirling around in graceful frozen stances, all with strange eyes looking beyond this world to some land far away from the rainbowed glitter of paint and lights in which they revolved.

The best time to sneak a ride was on a weekend in mid-summer when the beach was crowded and we could get lost in the sea of people overrunning the merry-go-round platform. Thrilling to the sounds of the mechanical band, we would get in a few slow revolutions before the ticket-taker spotted us and threw us off. It was hard for him not to notice the big black dog.

I would jump off my horse, dodge around the chariot pulled by three matching black horses, their necks stretched out, heads twisted forward and up in different directions, and Buster and I would go skidding off the turning stage, run down the ramp and off the pier, and then scoot under it. The ramp was a wide glittering entranceway with a great arch built over it with blinking lights spelling out "Old Orchard Beach."

> after dark
> the carousel horses glow
> more brightly

At night the pier was a passageway of lights out over the water, raised high in the air on giant pilings. Its entrance ramp began at the foot of the main street, just before the beach. The street came straight down a long hill, and was lined with hotels, restaurants and souvenir shops. In the shops, and out on the sidewalks, were pinwheels, toy shovels in picture-painted tin sandpails, and Old Orchard Beach pennants and post-cards. The hill ended about a hundred and fifty yards from the beach. In this level area—and spread along close to the shorefront on both sides of the street—were the railroad station and most of the larger amuse-ments: the roller coaster, bumper cars, rocket rides, loop-the-loops, an underground mine you rode through in a cart pulled by a real donkey, and various other rides, slides, fun houses, games of chance, and food and beverage stands. There was even another merry-go-round. At a large soda fountain, a silver spigot on a brass-hooped oak barrel spouted foamy drafts of ice-cold root beer. There were cotton-candy stands, a booth with scales where you got a prize if the man didn't guess your weight correctly, tattoo parlors, freak shows, and glass display-cases of elaborately carved, doll-sized figures that actually moved: a blacksmith shoeing a horse under a blossoming tree, people in a winter scene skating on a pond. There was a game where you threw baseballs to try and knock off the hats of life-size wooden clowns. As they moved across the stage their heads swiveled around and they raised and lowered their arms. Voices came from them, taunting the throwers.

> all the lights
> flare from the car fenders
> on the kiddy-ride

Lots more fun and games were off on side streets: there was a long stretch of rides and amusements called "The Great White Way," and there were many hotels, summer homes and cottages. Old Orchard was a famous resort in the 'twenties and 'thirties. Rudy Vallée and Fred Allen were headliners in the big hotels. My mother was a waitress in one of them for a while and sang occasionally with the hotel orchestra. Fred Allen heard her sing and promised her an audition if she came to New York.

Just before the pier's entrance ramp was the biggest funhouse at the beach: Noah's Ark. It was a great ship, as big as a three- or four-story house, perched high up over the street, and it rocked slowly back and forth from end to end. Life-sized comic figures and animals looked out of windows or stood on the deck or in doorways. They jerkily turned and bowed or nodded their heads or waved. Also near the ramp, but off to the side towards the sandy beach, there was always a bright red popcorn wagon.

The pier was very long. Its pilings carried it high above the beach and way out over the ocean. Even at low tide, the end of the pier was above many feet of water. And this was a gradually sloping beach, where the outgoing tide left vast stretches of sand uncovered. A glorious beach. Many of Maine's sandy beaches are broken by boulders and ledges or are only small stretches of sand between great cliffs. This beach went on for miles. Charles Lindbergh considered taking off from it to begin his transatlantic flight.

as we drive home
my father whistles a little tune
the dashlights glow

There were two large, partially enclosed pavilions on the pier, one at the beginning, holding the merry-go-round and souvenir and refreshment stands, and one at the end, that had a big penny arcade and a ballroom. Between them the pier was lined on both sides with booths: fried clams and french fries (with malt vinegar), candied-apple stands, ice cream cones, ring toss, fortune-tellers, and shooting galleries. There were balsam pillows and other souvenirs of Maine: maple-sugar candy, little birchbark canoes, and tiny carved seagulls standing on miniature pilings. At a photo booth you could put your head through a painted-set and be a circus strongman or a hula-hula dancer.

Here and there there were gaps between the concessions. These spaces might be only a foot or two wide, but on one side the booths ended completely for a long stretch of the pier, so people could look at the beach or the ocean as they strolled along. In this open area benches had been placed in front of the iron railings so your parents could rest from the excitement and wave to the people swimming in the water. Or Uncle Jim could sit down and enjoy his cigar while we played a game of chance.

> between the ring toss
> and a fortune-teller's booth
> the summer sea

When on my own I always ended up at the penny arcade. With Buster trailing after me, I would go around to every peep-show machine in the place, and there must have been a hundred. They had titles like: "The Daring Stagecoach Robbery," "Exotic Dancers," and "Boxing Thrills." My favorites were the old cowboy movies. The glassed peephole had small shields like a horse's blinders coming up by your temples to keep the arcade lights out. I would look in to see if the light in the machine was still on. This would mean someone had put a penny in the machine and failed to crank, or turn, the handle, or had only cranked the movie partway through. I was working against heavy odds.

The movie was made up of photographs taken from the frames of the original silent films. These were on cards that flipped into view as you cranked the handle—flipping under the little light that came on when a penny was dropped in the slot. Once in a while I would find the light still on. Then I could watch Jack Dempsey raise his hand in triumph or see a flickering Tom Mix ride off into the sunset. If I had a penny I could see Tom catch the bad guys, save the girl, and then ride off into the sunset.

> peep-show machine
> a cowboy rides into the sunset
> as the light goes out

Leaving the pier, I would imagine I was riding off on the white horse from the merry-go-round. Heading down the beach, I was crossing a sandy desert somewhere west of the Pecos after helping Tom round up a gang of rustlers. I galloped across it with a kind of skipping run, clicking my tongue for hoofbeats, and urging on my horse by slapping my thigh. Coming off the desert, I passed by a roaring volcanic mountain (the roller coaster), turned into a darkening canyon (between two resort hotels) and rode home in the gathering dusk to the X-Bar-X Ranch with my faithful companion bounding by my side.

the cards' edges
in the dark peep-show machine
still glitter

2. Hideouts

One of my earliest memories is the smell of wood. During the first few years of my life we lived next to a lumberyard along the riverbank in Saco, Maine. I remember climbing over piles of boards and liking the smell of the raw wood. I've loved the smell of newly sawn wood ever since.

During that period a lot of things came in wooden packing crates. This was before plywood became popular, or perhaps before it had been invented, and many of these crates were made of very thin boards of pine, closely fitted together. We kids would occasionally get hold of a discarded crate and use it to play in—imagining it was anything from a castle to an outlaw's hideout. On a bright sunny day in summer when I was alone in such a wooden box the light would glow through the thin walls of pine to create a soft golden atmosphere around me that I almost wanted to live in forever. Mingled with it was the faint fragrance of pine.

dust motes
float through a ray of light
inside the empty crate

Even when I was a bit older, around ten or eleven, I still liked to find or create hideouts for myself. A place I could be all alone, away from everybody and everything. I used to find and clear out a space inside the dense hedge in our backyard or somewhere out in the woods and bushes behind the house, for we lived then out in the country. I once tried to build a treehouse in an old pine, but it never got further than being a rough platform on two large branches. Anyway, being up in the air didn't give me the sense of security I felt hidden away on the ground.

> through the culvert
> a circle of blue sky
> in a distant ditch

I was into my world of cowboys and Indians in those days and would often pretend I was a cowboy hiding from a band of outlaws, or a lone Indian off on a hunt in enemy territory. But sometimes it was just *my* place and I enjoyed having my own little hideaway in the wide world. I would take an old piece of carpet or a worn blanket from home and use that to cover the scraped out floor of my retreat and I would keep some special smoothed sticks there. A few I made into clubs or spears and some were just nicely shaped sticks I kept for how they looked or felt. I'd also have some rounded stones, or horse-chestnuts, or I might even bury a favorite marble there—well, not a *favorite*, that I would keep at home, but a nice marble, maybe a blue one, to be the resident treasure of the place.

> hideout in the woods
> my bow and arrows
> wait for me

As I got still older I would discover "secret" places deep in the woods where I found my now more romantically inclined imagination coloring them in a quite different way. There was a clear spring in a little wooded hollow where the evening sun would lean through the trunks of the pines and spill some light into an edge of the water and across the thick carpet of moss that surrounded it. Here I could dream that the most beautiful girl in the world was coming to meet me. She would show me all the wonders of love . . . and of s-e-x.

> under the covers
> with a glowing penlight
> "Beauties in High Heels"

But usually a hideout was just a place—a secret place—to crawl into and kind of disappear from the regular world. I could dream there, or peek out through peepholes and watch the rest of the world continue on, oblivious of my spying on it. There was a pleasing simplicity (and complicity?) about this being alone in nature (though I didn't think of it as "nature"), surrounded by living branches, and having no furniture or belongings, except a makeshift ground cloth and some sticks. I could imagine living like an Indian, or a hermit, using my sticks to make a fire and to get food. Though that dream has never come true, it has had an influence on my view of the world and on the way I have lived my life.

> someone is calling
> from the other side of the house
> a few summer clouds

3. The Circus

> country road
> a circus-poster tiger
> in the spring rain

The circus in Dover, New Hampshire, where we moved when I began the fourth grade, was always in a huge field across the road from Gages Farm. It usually came to town towards the end of summer, but the posters appeared long before the circus. I would get up early the day it was to arrive and go down to the field along with other local boys. We'd try to get a job helping out as we watched the circus people put up the tents. "Hey Mister, can I help do that?" You might help pull out the folds of a tent while it was still on the ground, or pull on the ropes to raise it, or be sent to water the animals, or be asked to carry things from one place to another. Once I was even allowed to help pound the stakes for the ropes holding up the tents. For our work we'd get a ticket to the "Big Top."

> from the tent
> a clown looks out
> at a scarecrow

I especially remember the grass. It was a marvel to me the way the circus grew out of that grassy field. The tents would go up and inside and outside there were fields of grass. But under the muted light that came glowing through the canvas the inside field had a strange enchantment about it.

a morning breeze blows under the circus tent

The grass soon got pushed and matted down from all the activity, especially at the entrances, but in one corner of a sideshow tent you might still see a daisy nodding. Or just beyond the fat woman's tent a couple of thistles would show blue against the bottom of the giant canvas banner that pictured her several times life-size.

a canvas sign
billows in the wind
"The Fat Lady"

rising over
the freak-show tent
a gibbous moon

Carrying water to the elephants, camels and other animals made me feel I'd been brought into contact with distant places around the world—places in Africa and Asia. The smells and sounds as well as the look of these animals brought a new sense of the earth into my life: its variety and novelty seemed endless.

straw
on the elephant's back
summer breeze

holding his Stetson
the circus cowboy wipes his brow
with the back of his sleeve

The circus often had a wild-west show. This was the part I liked best. Perhaps some of the acrobats doubled as cowboys, or even Indians, but they all seemed real to me—a world apart from the clowns and lion tamers. As the Indians on horseback dashed into the arena in pursuit of a stagecoach, throwing up dust from a New England field that had just turned into a western prairie, they were in turn chased by a galloping posse of sixgun-shooting cowboys, and the "Wild West" was here—now—right in front of me.

during the Wild-West show
the setting sun lights the posts
of the empty corral

The main show in the Big Top always started with the grand parade.
All the people and animals of the circus entered, many were decked out
in elaborate costumes with great feathered plumes and blazing colors.
The elephants, horses, camels, lions, tigers, dogs, and clowns, and all
the other performers, marched around the inside of the tent and out
again and then the ringmaster came out alone in the spotlight and with
a fanfare the circus began.

the ringmaster enters
all the horns of the band
point skyward

When the same thing was happening in all three rings under the big
top a magical feeling of mirroring or recreating swung the mind with
wonder. Our eyes would go from one circle to the other mesmerized by
several trick horses going around and around in each one. There would
be slight variations in these duplications and in the man or woman with
their long stick-like whips in the center of each circle, but these only

added to the magic spell. The center circle might be made up of all white horses. In the outer circles, they might be all black in one and all brown in the other. These trim and graceful creatures would all in unison change from single file to side-by-side, from trotting to galloping to walking to prancing to rearing up. They would all at once, on cue, swing about and circle in the opposite direction, their heads all nodding in rhythm with their pace. They had colorful cockades sticking up from their foreheads that nodded also.

Then would come the bareback riders in every ring. Each dazzling princess in tights rode standing on the back of a circling horse. Then she would stand on her hands and do acrobatics on top of the horse as it ran around and around, head bobbing to the sound of the circus band. Then the high wire acts. Then the trapeze artists. Then the lion tamers. And all the time the clowns running and falling and flapping and playing tricks on each other.

Then there would be a grand finale with a man being shot from a cannon or a tightrope star performing the most daring feat ever attempted on the high wire. It seemed like it could go on forever. But suddenly it was all over. The colors and sounds were gone and there was only a big crowd moving out of the tent, leaving behind a disarray of soda cups and flattened popcorn boxes.

Autumn

Autumn is the wind . . . and football. A football thrown downfield in a bullet-like spiral or kicked end over end through long slanting rays of sunlight. Autumn is a chill in the air, the rustle of leaves, the sound of a cricket. Going back to school. The smells of new pencil-boxes and textbooks. The wind. It's sweaters and jackets, new shoes or sneakers. It's going to the barber's, wetting your hair to get it to stay down, wishing your ears didn't stick out. The wind. The itchy feeling under your shirt and sweater after a hard game of football and you're walking home in the cold evening air knowing you'll be late for supper. Helping your father put on the storm windows. The wind. It's the reds and yellows fluttering through the woods as you run on the old woods-road before breakfast dreaming of becoming a champion long-distance runner. It's county fairs and pumpkins. Halloween and Thanksgiving. Grasses and bushes turning browns and greys and blacks, tangled shadows where the woodchuck disappears for the winter. The wind.

> tree-lined road
> from out of the autumn leaves
> comes a yellow schoolbus

leaves blowing
past the school windows
my row of cursive a's

tomato soup after school
my mother continues ironing
in the kitchen

the light from the garage
rustling leaves blow across
the driveway

far down field
the punt bounces in and out
of long afternoon shadows

playing in the rain
the pebbly feel of the football
as I get ready to pass it

throwing the football
it twirls through the drizzle
spinning off water

the receiver reaches . . .
with a splash, the football falls
in the wet grass

1. Football Season

Fall was football. As the weather got chilly, the sky a frostier blue, and the winds started whipping up around our collars, we put on a sweater or a light jacket—and someone would get out a football. Then we would start the ball twirling between us, spinning it through the cold air like a slow-motion bullet. (Though we sometimes threw it so it wobbled like a duck with one wing.) When receiving the ball we ran away from the thrower, looking back over our shoulder. Or we would run out and suddenly cut to either side. When we were throwing we would often run to one side and leap up into the air, sending the ball flying over our opponents' heads to intersect the path of the running receiver.

> long pass
> hands and ball come together
> in the end-zone sunlight

For me, one of the signs it was time to get out the "old pigskin" was the horsechestnuts dropping from the trees. Lying on the ground under the leaf-turning branches, half out of their prickly, thorny shells, the rich brown nuts, almost like polished wooden stones, were prized for their shape and color and size—and for their use as projectiles. After drilling a hole in one and threading a string through it, we could then whirl it rapidly around our heads and hurl it great distances, or whirling it in front of us, we could send it straight up to touch the clouds . . . and then dodge it as it came rocketing back down. We would sometimes collect the ammunition for these games on our way to or from the football field. Meanwhile the leaves of other trees were turning into the colors of autumn and flying through the air.

> the cheerleaders
> wave their pom-poms
> then their legs

The only "official" football team I ever played for was the high school junior varsity my sophomore year and I played for them on the bench. However I did get lots of experience during practice playing against the starters: learning what it feels like to put on a helmet, shoulder and thigh pads, and cleats. It made you feel bigger than life, armored like a knight. And then you hunkered down close to the ground at the line of scrimmage, dug in your cleats, and drove into the opposing line as if you and your fellow linesmen were a battalion of tanks.

But most of my football was played out of uniform and only for fun. In an unused pasture, a grass-grown field near Willand's Pond on the Somersworth Road, we would have our pick-up games of football. Though we sometimes played touch, we usually played tackle. Our bodies would soon be sore with bruises from banging against each other and the ground, and our faces would get scratchy, itchy and hot from being rubbed and scraped on the rough grasses of the field.

> pick-up game
> after the tackle everyone
> brushes off leaves

In the cold air of autumn, these physical aches and sores, combined with the sweating, breathless exertion of the game, only made us feel more alive—especially if we could break free of the pack, leap up into the crisp air of falling dusk and feel the smooth curves of the football slap into our outstretched hands and then be off to the end of the field with the winning touchdown.

> the tacklers get a sleeve
> but the kid slips from his sweater
> and runs for the touchdown

The energy we felt seemed to flow through us and the field and the surrounding woods. Though we didn't think about it as part of the energy flowing through the universe, we sensed there was some connection as we walked or biked home in the gathering dark and looked up at the stars coming out all over the autumn sky.

after the football game
kicking through leaves
to our bikes

2. Playing Alone: The Old Football

I lived out in the country in my teen years and there weren't too many kids my own age to play with—the nearest one lived over a mile away. So I often practiced baseball and basketball, and even football, by myself. In baseball, I wanted to be a catcher, so I practiced my throw to second base for hours in a field across the road from my house. Instead of trying to hit a second-baseman's glove, I tried to throw the ball into a pail placed on its side the regulation distance from home plate to second base. Making a perfect throw from behind the plate to catch a runner trying to steal second was one of life's great moments.

Basketball was the easiest game to practice by myself, because my father had helped me set up a basket and backboard in our backyard. Football was the most difficult. Though I could practice throwing a football into a pail—in this case setting it up on a box—this turned out to be quite hard, especially since most of the time I only had an old-fashioned football that was fatter around than the modern ball. I found it in our garage among some stuff that was there when my father bought the place. I was happy if I just managed to hit the pail and knock it off the box.

My favorite solo practice with that football was dropkicking it. Since it was the shape and size used back in the 'twenties it was easier to dropkick than the newer streamlined models. Maybe the changed shape of the ball was what caused dropkicking to go out of favor. The slimmer modern ball is hard to kick for extra points unless it is held still and place-kicked.

> tie score with seconds to go —
> in the backfield, the dropkicker
> extends his hands

I used to love to dropkick that old dark-colored, fat football—kicking it into the autumn sky until it got too dark to see it anymore. I can still picture it flying end over end, up and over the telephone wire that ran from a roadside pole over our lawn to the house.

After dropping the ball and as I kicked it—just as its point touched the ground—my hands would stretch straight out and upwards from my sides. As my right foot swung high into the air and reached the top of its arc my left foot would lift off the ground and for a moment I would be suspended in the sky, feeling a perfect part of it—with the ball flying straight and true into the chilly dusk.

> the football flies
> between the uprights
> with some autumn leaves

3. School

The things in school that seemed to speak to me of the wonder of existence were rarely the lessons I heard and read there. They were the things I touched, or smelled, or saw. Things that spoke through my senses directly to my feelings, my emotions, my being—that spoke to whatever is eternal in me. I know that now. Then I only felt it.

They were only everyday, ordinary kinds of things, that no one, particularly a child, would normally attribute much significance to—such as the smell of lunches left in the cloakroom. You might not notice how good the smell of apples and oranges, chicken or cheese sandwiches, cupcakes, celery stalks and raw carrot strips, peanut butter and Marshmallow Fluff could be unless you were sent to the cloakroom for being "bad." The lunches were placed there, on shelves, because if we kept them in our desks we might sneak a bite during class.

With the sun streaming through the window at one end of the shadowy long hallway-like "room," with hooks along both sides, amidst the coats and jackets that hung there, you had to stand and meditate. You were supposed to think about what you had done wrong and feel sorry about it, and determine to be better. But I usually daydreamed about having great adventures as a cowboy, or a knight of King Arthur's Round Table, or as an army commando sneaking up on Gestapo headquarters. Sometimes my mind just sort of emptied and I was just the lights and shadows of the long hall-room, or the dust motes shifting in the sunlight, or the subtle smells that came on wispy currents of air from the brown paper bags and lunchboxes placed along the shelves.

> quiet library
> sunlight on a wooden table
> at the end of the stacks

Another simple thing I got close to in school was the top of my wooden desk. Sometimes I just put my head down on it and felt the cool wood against my cheek. Or I would prop my elbow on it with my chin in my hand and study it. I would gaze at its gold-brown surface, and pass my other hand over the lines and whorls of the grain, feeling them with my mind—it was usually too smooth and varnished to actually feel them with your fingers. You could feel the carvings in its surface, however. And these too could give pleasure. Especially after you added your own initials and intertwined them with the charmed initials of the girl you loved, but could never tell. In fact, you could hardly talk to her at all. But you could feel her initials.

snow whirls outside
she looks at the glitter of stars
pasted on her paper

Then there was the world of the windows, or outside the windows. Those huge windows of the old schools, where the sky—perhaps blue-black and stormy, or a clear blue crossed by a small white cloud—always seemed to hang above a world much more interesting than the one you were in in the classroom: a world of sandlots, tar pits, fish ponds, and railroad yards. And the big clock on the wall moved its hands so slowly you sometimes thought they didn't move at all.

darkening schoolroom
a partly furled flag
stands in a corner

There was also an enchantment about the large white globes that hung from the classroom ceiling on linked chains. These globes were not really spherical. They had a bowl-like shape, a bit wider at the top than at the bottom, with the upper and undersides almost flat—the underside flaring down slightly in the center to a rounded point. The milk-white glass glowed a soft, pale yellow when the bulb inside it was lit, but the light it shed was bright and cheerful.

> rainy day
> they turn the lights on
> in school

The lights were especially warm and washed with a kind of glory on dark, winter days—days of grey, drizzly rain and sleet—days when the lights were almost as necessary as if it were night. On bright sunny days, or most ordinary days, the classroom lights did not have to be turned on. The large windows let in more than enough light. This was probably what gave the lights their added attraction—that they were *not* always on. So that when they did come on, to hold back the daytime darkness, they glowed with a light that seemed friendly and secure. Somehow they even added a luster to the teacher's words.

> as she turns the pages
> a light comes and goes
> on her face

Recess was immensely popular. When the bell rang we often ran out into the schoolyard hollering with joy and if anyone asked us our favorite subject we (boys) always said "recess." But there were some special moments that had to do with learning. Like the time Miss Bullard told us about the Abenaki Indians and even gave me a book about them called *Indian Hero Tales*, which I still have. Or in Miss McCooey's class when I first worked out a geometric proof all by myself and it rounded out perfectly into its Q.E.D. as if it had been decreed by God, which in a sense I guess it had.

    moonlight
    pieces of chalk glow
    below the blackboard

Winter

Winter is snow . . . and basketball. Basketball in a real gym—the springy bounce of the polished wooden floors, the whisper of perfectly strung nets, the bright lights and high ceilings, the echo of the bouncing ball. Making a perfect shot—the prize of endless hours of practicing on outdoor courts. Winter is skating and skiing. Building snowforts with arsenals of snowballs. It's waiting in snowdrifts for the schoolbus, long days in school, coming home to a hot bowl of soup. It's closing the door quick because the snow is blowing in. Winter is the radio. It gets dark early and you come in out of the cold to lie on the living room rug in front of the big radio console and listen to adventure serials like *The Lone Ranger* or *Terry and the Pirates*. Winter is ice and icicles, fireplaces and frosted windows, the skittering of a last brown leaf over the snow crust. It's flying over the frozen pond on glittering skates, blowing your breath out in great plumes of mist, flashing to a stop in a wave of sparkling ice flecks. It's the cold yellow-grey sun so distant and slanting as it flickers at evening over the pines and across the snow-covered fields. It's great drifts of snow flowing through the woods, frosty stars shining on them, and mysterious bears sleeping beneath them. Christmas lights.

Tire chains clanking. Trucks spreading sand on the icy roads. A giant bank of snow thrown across the end of the driveway by the snowplow. Snowball fights and fist fights. Slush and fragments of dry sunny pavement. Waking to the silence and hushed light of the deepest snowfall in years. Making makeshift snowshoes from old tennis rackets and pretending to be an Indian on the warpath. Looking back at my tracks winding through the woods.

winter wind
the dog comes in with snow
stuck to his coat

home sick—
my mother feels my forehead
then fluffs my pillow

Monopoly in the kitchen
snow drips from the overshoes
in the entry

snowstorm at night
the enclosed porch lit
by the back-door window

turning out
all the lights but the ones
on the tree

after the long jump-shot
running back up court looking
for her face in the crowd

deep snow
a fielder's glove waits on the wall
of the gym office

1. The Radio, Big-Little Books, and the Movies

A big part of growing up a boy in the 'thirties and 'forties was listening to the radio serials: *Tom Mix*, *The Lone Ranger*, *Terry and the Pirates*, *Jack Armstrong The All American Boy*, and *Superman*. The westerns were my favorites. These programs were on early in the evening so some of them interfered with supper. Before I got into the seventh or eighth grade and sports became so important to me, I was home by dusk most evenings in the winter to be sure and hear Tom Mix and His Ralston Straight Shooters. While a blizzard blew snow around our house, I would be far away in a land of cactus and sagebrush. As Tom rode his black horse Tony through the hot desert or the rolling prairies of the southwest, I was riding along with him—watching a cloud of dust resolve itself into a band of Indians, or seeing the sun setting behind a distant butte, or noticing the moon rise above a canyon rim as we dismounted to sneak up on a rustlers' hideout cabin.

> lying on the floor
> listening to hoofbeats
> coming out of the radio

The Lone Ranger program began with the announcer saying, "From out of the past come the thundering hoofbeats of the great horse, Silver." Lying on the living room rug with my head near the large console with its glowing dial I would live the days of the early West with the Lone Ranger and Tonto until the final commercial came on and my mother called me into the kitchen for supper.

> Tonto tells us
> about the puffs of smoke
> rising in the distance

Big-Little books also inspired me with this love of cowboys and western landscapes. They were called "big" because they were thicker than most novels, almost 1 1/2 inches, and "little" because they were only 3 5/8 inches wide by 4 1/2 inches high. With few exceptions, all the left-hand pages were printed with text while all the right-hand pages had a one panel comic-book-like drawing. Instead of the dialogue balloons used in comic books, there were one-line captions under each panel.

Some of the pictures in the Big-Little books had the simplicity of Japanese sumie art. In black and white, with restrained use of line and usually with lots of white space, these small drawings were surprisingly evocative in getting the mind to fill in the details. For a night scene there might be a range of mountains outlined on white space with a patch of black in the upper-right corner for the sky. In this black space hung a circle of white—the full moon.

The one-line captions under these pictures were taken or adapted from the accompanying text, and sometimes had the concise suggestiveness of a haiku, a kind of writing I would not know about for years to come. The covers were of stiff cardboard, smooth-finished and brightly colored. The featured cowboy was often pictured in a close-up on the cover wearing a large cowboy hat. Though cowboy big-little books were the most treasured, especially Buck Jones and Tom Mix, I also liked Dick Tracy, Tarzan The Ape Man, and Flash Gordon. I loved these small books more than comic books and collected them in the late 'thirties when I was seven and eight years old and still living in Maine.

> the big-little book
> Tom Mix looks out from the shadow
> of his ten-gallon hat

The game of "Cowboys and Indians" was played year-round in those early years. We would pack six-shooter cap-guns in leather holsters or wear a feathered headband and carry a bow and arrows, break up into small bands and chase each other around the neighborhood and nearby woods. Once, I got my mother to buy me a blue Buck Jones shirt that had white horseshoes embroidered on the collar flaps and a white string tying up the opening at the neck just like Buck's. Besides the big-little books about cowboys I was also reading Zane Grey novels, Fran Striker's adventure novels about The Lone Ranger, and a series about two teen-age cowboys, called "The X-Bar-X Boys." And then there were the cowboy movies.

> rainy Saturday
> in front of the movies
> the wet posters

My first movie, at the age of four or five, was a cowboy movie. My father took me to see a Buck Jones' film at a theater in Biddeford, Maine, and I at once fell in love with the Old West. After we moved from Maine to the outskirts of Dover, New Hampshire, in the fall of 1940, when I was nine, I would hike—sometimes hitchhiking on snowy or rainy days—the three or four miles in to the State Theater on Saturday mornings to see the weekly cowboy movies. They might be showing a Ken Maynard cattle-rustling film or a Johnny Mack Brown shoot-em-up, a Hopalong Cassidy sagebrush thriller or a Gene Autry singing-cowboy adventure—or a movie starring any number of other ten-gallon-hatted heros of the silver screen.

The feature was always preceded by a chapter of a serial, usually also a western. One exciting serial, with Wild Bill Elliott playing Wild Bill Hickok, had lots of Indian scenes and Wild Bill seemed to be always leaping on or off his horse or riding through the wildest of the Wild West. He rode a lively pinto that was colorful even in black and white and which still gallops across the plains of my imagination.

> movie serial
> the stagecoach goes off a cliff
> end of chapter one

Coming out of the theater when it was still the middle of the day with your mind full of rearing horses, cattle herds, and runaway stagecoaches made for a strange way of looking at the reality around you. Even under a cold and gloomy winter sky, the buildings and stores along the street of a small New England city would become saloons and blacksmith shops in a sun-baked western town. Over there was the sheriff's office and there was "The Last Chance Hotel." A streak of sand in the gutter might become a streak of gold in a mountain stream. Or I would stand at the edge of the curb and be looking out from a mountain ledge at the stagecoach route to Dodge City. What *is* that cloud of dust?

2. Hockey

After Willand Pond froze over and the ice got thick enough to hold us we would get out our skates and go play hockey. Some years the pond froze in strong winds and the ice was all ridged and bumpy—which ruined the skating. Most of the time it froze as smooth as glass. Then the wind might keep patches of it swept clear of snow for us. But usually we had to shovel the snow off the ice to make a place to skate. I still remember trudging under the snow-covered pines down to the frozen pond through long, wavy drifts with both a shovel and a hockey stick over my shoulder, my hockey skates dangling from the stick.

> the frozen pond
> trying to follow the kids
> the dog slips six ways

The pond was completely surrounded by woods. So we felt we were in the wild, though there were some houses on the small, dirt roads off the west side of the pond. To mark each goal, we placed two stones, or somebody's jacket and hat, on the ice and we had to get the puck between them. Even if the weather was freezing, it was a hot game. We would be huffing and puffing great clouds of smoky breath into the cold air, and working up a sweat under our sweaters, as we flashed and crashed from one end of our improvised rink to the other.

> flipping the puck
> into the air and over the ice
> the faraway sun

When not playing a game, and if the whole pond was clear, we would swirl and glide on our skates for great distances across the glittering ice, almost flying. The pond was about a mile from one end to the other. Out in the middle the ice would look black and we knew we were skating over great depths of water. When the freezing ice expanded, there would be deep booming sounds and long, tight cracks would streak across a vast stretch of the pond.

Here and there holes were chopped in the ice for ice-fishing. We could see that the ice was about a foot thick. The line going into the hole was rigged to a thin bent stick with a small red flag. When a fish pulled on the line a trigger released the stick, raising the flag so it flew a few feet above the ice.

> bitter wind
> a red flag flies above
> the ice-fishing hole

Going home afterwards, again earthbound, our feet would feel clumsy and leaden pushing through the snow. The racing of our blood that came from the rushing swiftness of the skating gradually slowed. It would be dark by the time we quit, and the stars came out as we trudged back into the shadows of the pines.

        moonrise
        the hole in the ice
        refreezes

3. Basketball Season

Winter was basketball. Even before the first snowfall, I would begin to think of trying to get into a gym to play basketball. I remember traveling all the way to Portsmouth once to play in a gym. A group of us got together from Dover and challenged a Portsmouth team in some kind of league they had over there. The seaport of Portsmouth wasn't all that far from Dover, but it seemed far in those days when none of us kids had a car. One boy managed to borrow the panel truck from his father's cleaning business.

I've never forgotten the game that day, because I couldn't miss. It was as if I had an extra-sensory power that found a direct path through the air to the basket even with my head turned away. All I had to do was put the ball on it. I don't remember how many points I made that day but it seemed like a hundred. My hookshot went up and in from all parts of the court. We creamed them.

> cold morning
> in the empty basketball gym
> the blank scoreboard

Though I never made the high school team, I still managed to play some pick-up games in the high school gym, or in some of the church gyms in Dover. In one small gymnasium in a church basement the ceiling was only two feet above the basket. You had to zip the ball in on a very low trajectory. When I couldn't get into a gym, I would play in my backyard where I had a basket and backboard, or I'd play wherever there was a basket: in front of somebody's garage or in a playground. We played in wind and rain, in snow and sleet. With freezing hands a few of us would play until dark—and sometimes after dark. I could play in my backyard by the light over the back porch.

But there was no matching the feeling you got in a real gymnasium. The sound of the ball bouncing on the gleaming wood floors. The elastic feel of the boards under your sneakered feet. The lights and the warmth, the clean bright airiness, and the way the ball would whisper through a basket's strings when the net was not torn, or imagined—but all there.

> starry night
> sounds of basketball practice
> from the gym

My senior year in high school I was cut from the basketball squad again, so I joined the National Guard in Dover and played for their team. I got to use the Armory gym almost any afternoon after school that I wanted to. Sometimes, especially if the weather was bad—a big snowfall or a freezing blizzard—I had the gym all to myself and I would practice my hookshot or my lay-ups for hours at a time.

There was a warm, lonely feeling to be in the gym on a rainy, sleety day in winter all by yourself. Outside was gray, windy, and cold. Inside was bright and the blonde wood of the floor would look warm even if the gym was a little chilly. Jumping around and running in and out to the basket warmed you up anyway. And the sound of the ball kept you company in a strange way, the echoing bounce when dribbling, or the few bounces before taking a practice foul-shot. The rebounding thuds off the backboard, or the "spang" off the rim—or the swish and faint snap of the net's strings when the ball fell through the hoop without touching the rim. A little moment of perfection.

> at the foul line
> bouncing and bouncing the ball
> then the pause

Basketball can be played as a game of solitude more easily than most other team sports. In baseball, for instance, you really need someone else to throw the ball with you. In basketball it can be just you and the ball playing together for hours. You catch or chase it when it rebounds from the basket or backboard, sometimes even calling to it. You practice dribbling and it circles all around you. Taking it with you on a fast dribble to the basket for a lay-up, you rise together into the air and then you let it go up against the board, giving it just the right twist to bank it into the hoop.

> deep winter
> I spin the basketball
> on one finger

The long arc of a hookshot from out to the side of the foul line, the ball rising up from behind my head as I turned to look at the basket, was, when it worked just right, like creating a feat of magic, like being a flawless part of our planet's passage through space, matching the smoothness and the spinning accuracy of its looping around the sun. The concentration on the basket—to just put the ball in it—was almost like concentrating on a mantra or a candleflame during meditation. The mind cleared. My hands, my eyes, my whole body and mind leaped towards the basket and went with the ball up and through the hoop. Into a circle of nothingness.

> while it snows
> I sink a hookshot in the gym
> the swish of the net

The Paper Route

The Paper Route

Winter 1944-45   Dover, New Hampshire

the road after dark
on either side, giant snowbanks
left by the plow

far-apart streetlights
leaving one walking towards
another

singing to the icy moon
"I got spurs that jingle, jangle, jingle"
while folding a newspaper

passing the warm windows
on the way to a back door
the freezing wind

putting a newspaper in the entry
I hear the girl with the ringlets
laughing inside

on the plowed road
the packed snow squeaks
under my boots

the darkness between houses
I dream of the young widow
wearing only her slip

a closed porch
leaving the paper in cold shadows
inside the storm door

dark house
a dog barks inside
as I drop the evening paper

shadows under the pines
the Tom Mix decoder-badge
in my pocket

through the frosted pane
Mr. Slate by his console radio
pinning flags on a wall map

putting the newspaper
on a small snowdrift
between the doors

another dark house
the stillness as the moon
goes behind a cloud

dodging around a snowbank
I sink a long shot
for the silent stars

taking a short-cut
and getting snow in my boots
my crooked trail

Old Man Smith
hollering inside
his dog snarling out back

shooting one of the Murphy gang
as he rides out of ambush
from behind Smith's garage

someone working in his cellar
the light shines out
on shovelled snow

uncleared driveway
just visible in a dark window
the gold star flag

Mrs. Turner comes to the door
with last week's money
the light curves around her breasts

the snowy field
where we played baseball
a falling star

sounds of supper
I shut the door quietly
on the evening news

wind in the cemetery
snowdrifts around the headstones
swirl into ghosts

walking quickly
past the crazy woman's farm
a stamping in the barn

deserted crossroads
the stop sign almost buried
under drifts

unplowed street
a single set of footprints
through the snow

the war safe in my bag
the moon and stars shine down
on the frozen pond

A Boy's Fights

A Boy's Fights

1. The First Fight

It happened in the first grade, shortly after I read a picture book about Ferdinand the Bull. I remember a picture of Ferdinand lying contentedly under his cork tree in the middle of a flowery meadow.

I was very taken with Ferdinand and his philosophy of life. As you may recall, this friendly, nature-loving bull was a pacifist. I don't think he called himself one or thought of himself that way. Perhaps he just wanted to be peaceful and quiet. Taken from his uneventful but happy life in the meadow, he was dragged to the bullring to fight with a matador. He also had to contend with picadors, padded horses, and other brightly-costumed tormentors. He sat down in the middle of the ring and refused to do battle with anyone or anything. He was certainly not going to attack a piece of red cloth. Instead, he smelled a flower that someone had thrown into the ring. Nothing they did could change his mind. The details have faded from my memory, but I do know that he was eventually allowed to return to his flower-filled field and lived happily ever after under his cork tree.

across the field
from out of a bunch of cows
comes something bigger

towering clouds
through the Queen Anne's Lace
the bull's pace quickens

back over the fence
behind me the trotting bull swerves
then stands quietly

I thought Ferdinand's attitude towards violence showed a certain nobility of spirit and his being allowed to return to his life among the flowers a just resolution to the story. I praised him as a hero to my schoolmates and asked them to call me Ferdinand. Immediately, I ran into a storm of opposition. Since my real name was Cornelis and they all had fun calling me "Corny," they were sputteringly hostile to any change. And, they shouted, with a few dirty words thrown in for emphasis, Ferdinand was a sissy and a coward for not goring and trampling the matador, and I was more of the same for praising him.

By the end of the day I was at bay at the edge of the schoolyard before five or six boys who were all jeering at me for my backing of good old Ferdinand. Gaining courage from their number, two of them began shoving and pushing me. To uphold the ideals and way of life of my hero I started to walk away, out of the schoolyard, and down the road. The yard was dirt, but the road was mostly gravel, with a fair number of rocks and pebbles scattered here and there. When I was about twenty feet down the road, one of the pushers, a second-grader, made the mistake of picking up a rock and throwing it at me.

This didn't strike me as fair and I quickly gathered a supply of several good-sized rocks and headed back toward the taunting Ferdinand-haters. A number of them were now also picking up stones and preparing to let go at me. With missiles flying all around me, I advanced steadfastly towards my foes and with unerring aim dispatched two of them with hits to a shoulder and a head.

This development—plus the fact that their throws all missed me—seemed to dishearten them, and one and all they adopted the strategy of Ferdinand and refused to fight any longer. In fact, they fled the field, following the initiator of the rock-throwing, who had run away screaming as soon as my stone bounced off his head.

winter moon
the stillness of the rocks
on the gravel road

I don't recall how I reconciled my actions with the peaceful ideals I had been advancing to the other kids but I do remember feeling I had somehow proven my point.

2. The Second Fight

My next big fight was six or seven years later, but there were some brief fights at the beginning of the fourth grade that had to do with a change in my identity. I had attended the first grade in Old Orchard Beach, Maine, when we lived at the Half-Way, a crossroads between the beach and Saco. We then moved to Saco. I can't think of any fights in the second grade there, or in the third grade, when we lived on a farm in Scarborough and I went to a two-room schoolhouse with four grades in each room. By the fourth grade we were living in Dover, New Hampshire. Moving around so much in my early years made it difficult to acquire any lasting friends. So I had to start out alone each year, finding myself surrounded by strangers who delighted in making fun of my name, which was still officially Cornelis, after my Dutch grandfather.

in the schoolyard
his hat goes from boy to boy
trying not to chase it

crack-the-whip
whirling off the end he knocks down
the kid who took his hat

the kid
who first grabbed his hat
now his best friend

After the usual kidding around about my name at the beginning of the fourth grade at Sawyer School in Dover in the fall of 1940, I realized that I must take drastic action or this might go on for the rest of my life. I decided to give myself a new name. Something that would sound like a regular nickname. One that had a bit of a tough ring to it, yet would still fit me. I was not a Spike or Butch. Since I was half Dutch—my father was from Holland—I would call myself "Dutchy."

This seemed a good choice to me for a number of reasons. First, my father had occasionally been called Dutchy since he left Holland. (His real name was Dirk but he Americanized it and he was known as Dick by almost everyone including my mother, who was from Scotland. At school, we shortened our last name to be more American. So my little brother whose real name was Dirk Jan van den Heuvel, like our father's, was called Dickie Heuvel.) Second, when we had the farm in Scarborough, my father put out a sign above our roadside stand on Route 1 that said "Dutchy's Vegetables & Eggs." But the third reason, and the real clincher for choosing my new name, was that it was almost the same nickname used by one of the toughest, most notorious gangsters of the time, Dutch Schultz.

So I announced one day in the schoolyard that from now on my name would be Dutchy, and it only took one or two brief fistfights to make it stick. Soon everyone, except my mother and a few teachers, called me Dutchy.

> writing his nickname
> in all his favorite books
> and on his baseball glove

I never looked for fights, and true to my old hero Ferdinand I usually tried to avoid them. Through the years there had been the occasional bumping of chests and even some shoving and a few punches, but no really going at it with all stops out, that I remember, until that wrestling match with my friend Donald on the wooded hill behind Foss's house, the summer between the sixth and seventh grades. We had been playing cowboys and Indians out in the woods and in a lull after I'd hit him a little too hard in the make-believe battle, he said something about my grandfather.

> cops and robbers
> pretending to fight turns
> into the real thing

Neither of us had ever seen this grandfather, David Yuill, my mother's father. He was in Scotland. His wife, taking their two daughters with her, had left him years ago because he drank too much. She decided to go to New Zealand. She could only afford to take the youngest girl, Mary, with her. So, my mother, Lily, was left behind in Glasgow. At the age of fourteen, she was placed "in service," and became a maid for a rich family.

A few years later she went to Canada where she met my father. They married and moved to Maine after a honeymoon in Holland. All this because her father, Davy Yuill, a cornet player in a Glasgow band, used to get drunk and come home and make life unbearable for his wife and children.

I had heard a number of family stories about Davy and his problems with drink. Also that he had been gassed in the Great War and had received a medal and a silver cornet for bravery. (My mother forgave him for the troubles he had caused her and sent him care packages of food and clothing during and after the World War II "Blitz" of Britain.) I had made the mistake of confiding some of this family history to my pal, Donald.

the Monopoly game ends
with a robbery of the bank
and scattered houses

He was a year younger than me but he was tough and wiry and almost as big as me. He was always on the go, always testing himself and others. He liked to accept and give challenges, daring you to walk over a crossbeam two stories high in an old crumbling mill or to leap from a high cliff into a sandbank. And Donald was almost always willing to go first.

He played baseball and football in the pick-up games we had and he liked to go skiing. He also liked to try unusual sports—at least they were fairly unusual where we lived—like pole-vaulting, cross-country running, and wrestling. He even got me and a few others interested in them.

> pole vaulting
> following my feet into the sky
> letting go

Anyway, he challenged me by insulting my grandfather. And, of course, though I had never known this grandfather and had been told by my own mother that he drank to excess, I felt duty-bound to defend his name. He *was* my grandfather! I forgot my hero Ferdinand—and one of my mother's favorite sayings: "Sticks and stones may break your bones, but names will never hurt you."

It was always a more serious insult to have your mother or father called names than to be called names yourself. A grandfather was an extension of this principle. You were more duty-bound to defend the family's honor than your own. I forget exactly what Donald had said. He probably called him a drunk. Whatever it was, I said he would have to take it back, and he of course said no.

Donald loved to wrestle, so it was hard to stand toe to toe and just slug it out. He would always try to slip around you and get you in a half- or full-nelson, or try to trip you up and get a hammerlock on you. We'd wrestled for fun before, usually in front of my house.

> a butterfly
> flies over the wrestling boys
> the half-mowed lawn

So we wrestled up and down that hill in the woods for about a half-hour or more, scrabbling through bushes, rolling up against the trunk of a pine tree, and generally getting all bruised, scratched, hot, sweaty, itchy, and sore. Different grips were punctuated with such cries as "Take it back," "I won't!" and "He is so!" "He isn't!"

At one point he had me in a hammerlock, twisting my arm and pushing it higher and higher behind my back. I went over in a somersault, pulling him down with me. I scrambled around and got a scissors-hold with my legs around his waist and started squeezing him. I also grabbed his head and tried to turn it around backwards. He managed to get hold of one of my feet and bent it the wrong way. At the same time he wriggled and shook himself loose, rolling part way down the hill.

We both stood up and stared at each other, red-faced and panting. We took deep gulps of air trying to catch our breaths. Then Donald dove for my feet, toppling me over, and we were off again.

> "go on home
> your mother's callin' ya"
> "oh yeah?"

He may have finally allowed the old man wasn't all that bad and I may have admitted he took a drop too much, but I kind of doubt it. I don't really remember. He probably stuck to his guns and continued to insist that his characterization of my grandfather was the right one.

When we'd wrestled other times as a kind of game, one or both of us would occasionally get mad and things could take a more serious turn. But we usually worked out a truce and didn't stay mad at each other long. In this case we finally stopped wrestling and somehow cooled off. Perhaps we just got tired of fighting and straggled home.

taking the dare—
from the top of the telephone pole
seeing for miles around

3. The Third Fight

The biggest fight I ever had in school was in the eighth grade. It took place because of something *I* said. I didn't usually have a big mouth. In fact, at that time I was a quiet, mind-his-own-business, rather shy kind of kid. But when I did happen to say something it too often turned out to be the wrong thing. It had happened enough times in the past year that I had recently chosen for my hero a figure out of the history of the Netherlands famous for keeping his mouth shut: William the Silent.

He led the war of liberation for the Dutch against the Spanish in the 16th Century. I'd learned about him in John Lothrop Motley's *The Rise of the Dutch Republic* while reading about my Dutch heritage. He was the hero of the war even though he didn't live to see the final victory for freedom. He only spoke when it was necessary. And then spoke only words that revealed his great heart and mind.

> at recess
> he imitates the teacher
> who's right behind him

It was the beginning of the summer of 1945 and another war, World War II, seemed to be almost over. It had just ended in Europe and the Japanese were in retreat in the Pacific. A warm afternoon in early June in Dover. With some of the other kids in my eighth grade class I was decorating the classroom for our coming graduation from grade school.

One of my friends, Arthur, now had a steady girlfriend. While we were up on stepladders hanging some crepe-paper streamers I opened my big mouth and said something stupidly unkind about the girl. I can't even remember now what it was.

Arthur got rightfully red-faced and angry. I'd put him in a spot where he had to defend the honor and virtue of his girl. He promptly challenged me to a fight, to start when school was out. Now, upholding the code of honor was in my corner. I had to accept or be branded a coward. Though I regretted what I'd just said, it would do no good to take it back—that would be seen only as a sign that I was afraid to fight.

> the boy in love
> he scowls at anyone who dares
> speak her name

So here I was trying to be a man of few words, and those words must be pearls of wisdom. Silence itself is golden. But right out of the golden stillness of a June afternoon, I stupidly blurt out something I think—without thinking—is funny. And so end up having to fight someone I'd actually like to keep as a friend.

> lined up to enter school
> the last kid pokes the next:
> "pass it on"

We were about the same size and weight: slim, tall for our age, and in good shape. We were active in sports and both had paper routes. Arthur was into boxing. Often that winter and spring, we'd gone on lunch hour to his place two blocks from school with several other boys to spar on the second floor of the garage, actually an old, small barn, behind his house. He'd made it into a gym. With real boxing gloves we would have boxing matches with each other. There was a large, stuffed body-bag to develop our hooks, straight jabs, and power punches. And a regular punching bag on which we could practice short rapid-fire rotating jabs in a rhthym that would set the bag snapping back and forth in a blur of motion. There was a heavy medicine ball to throw around, and even rope for skipping. We would have workouts just like the pros did in the movies we saw at the Strand.

> Jimmy Cagney
> watches the sparring in the gym
> and sneers

It was during one of these boxing matches in Arthur's barn that I learned the expression "seeing stars" when you got knocked out was really true. This phenomenon was graphically illustrated in the comics by showing stars spinning in a circle around the head of anyone that got K.O.'d. Someone tagged me with a solid right to the side of the head: everything went black and I felt my knees buckling. As I was going down, the blackness filled with bright and sparkling stars.

Though I felt frightened by the sudden darkness, the stars fascinated me and I remember being pleasantly surprised and amazed, amidst my fear, at how brilliant and intense they were. I'm not sure I was really out—but if I was it was for only a few seconds. It was enough to give me an idea of how powerful a blow from a fist, even padded with a boxing glove, could be. I determined to keep my guard up.

> summer heat
> the dog and cat both lie
> under the front porch

The day was still getting hot as we dutifully met that afternoon on the lawn next to Arthur's house. In fact we walked over from school together after he said goodbye to his girlfriend. She was a pretty girl with long, attractive black hair, who would later become a cheerleader in high school. She knew nothing about our argument.

His parents were not home and Arthur decided we would go at it bare-knuckles right there on the lawn. No civilizing boxing gloves or set rounds. This was a duel to the death. However, he insisted on a kind of ceremony to initiate his vendetta. I must knock a chip, actually a twig, off his shoulder to show I wasn't afraid of meeting his challenge. "I dare you to knock it off!" was the ritualistic phrase he hurled at me. I responded by moving forward with my left hand up before my face and my right extended toward him. I flipped the twig off his left shoulder and it flew across the lawn.

We went at it warily at first. Dancing around each other, we tried to feel out each other's weaknesses. We didn't sink to any unseemly wrestling or shoving, no trying to get headlocks around the neck or grabbing and rolling on the ground. We settled down toe to toe and began to slug it out.

I felt a kind of crunching as my fist bounced off his cheekbone, then felt a stabbing sting in my mouth. I started to bleed from a split lip. I sucked at it to keep it from dripping on my clothes and kept on fighting.

We banged and cuffed at each other on that lawn for about half an hour. We began to slow down a bit, but neither of us was ready to quit— "cry uncle" or "throw in the towel," as we called it in those days.

One of us remembered we had to get our newspapers at Foster's (*Foster's Daily Democrat*) and go on our paper routes. We had already stayed late at school to help with the decorating and now it was about the time we usually picked up our papers from the printing plant behind the newspaper office on the lower square.

It was more than half a mile from Arthur's house on Sixth Street to the office. We had to go out to and along Central Avenue into town past the railroad station, through the upper square, then down the hill and across the Cocheco River and after several more blocks to the lower square.

> sparrows by the falls
> the old brick shoe factory hums
> with wartime activity

Since neither of us would give up we decided to move the fight downtown. We gradually moved out onto the sidewalk, taking turns backing out to Central Avenue and then down the avenue towards the upper square, pounding at each other all the way.

We both now had cuts on our faces and I noticed that Arthur's left eye was beginning to look dark and puffy. We fought hard but we fought fair, having been taught by Hopalong Cassidy and The Lone Ranger. These Saturday-matinee and radio-serial cowboy heroes inspired us with the desire to be straight-shooters just like them, reinforcing the Golden Rule—"Do unto others as you would have them do unto you"—that we had learned about in Sunday School.

> collecting scrap metal
> Boy Scouts in a big truck
> shout war slogans

As we got closer to the railroad crossing and station, we realized we would soon have to halt our progress for awhile, because there was a long train stopped there. The gates were down and traffic was backed up on Central Avenue waiting for the train to move.

We kept moving steadily onwards, still fighting and both fairly tattered-looking sights. Our sleeves were rolled up, shirt-tails hanging out, and our pants were scuffed at the knees where we had gone down temporarily from one blow or another. It was hot in the sun and our faces were streaked with blood and sweat.

Above the grunting and the sound of whacks we gave and received we began to notice a kind of roaring sound like the shouting voices of a crowd. We stole a quick look ahead and saw hundreds of soldiers leaning out of the windows of the train. It was a troop train and it seemed as if the whole United States Army was cheering us on.

More and more soldiers joined those already leaning from every window on our side of the train and the shouting became as loud as that at a real sporting event.

I'm afraid we really lost our tempers now, neither wanting to be shown up in front of America's heroes, each wanting to be the Army's champion. The suddenly renewed pummeling became so intense that we ended up flinging each other to the ground. Then we began rolling in the dirt at the edge of the sidewalk, losing the bit of dignity we'd preserved up till then.

The soldiers went wild. About half of them cheered me on while the other half cheered for Arthur. While we rolled around, first one on top then the other, the train began to move. As it headed down the track, the shouting voices began to fade off into the distance. They were applauding now as well as cheering. Then they were gone.

far down the tracks
the train wavers in the heat
then fades into it

We got up as the gates rose, straightened ourselves up a bit, walked across the tracks, and resumed our boxing match. We continued to battle all the way along the upper square and partway down the hill towards the river, stopping at a public drinking fountain on the street corner just before Newberry's Five and Ten Cent store.

We had a momentary truce while we washed the blood and sweat off our itching and stinging faces and took several long, cool drinks of water while standing there on the hot sidewalk.

small town afternoon
a cook throws scraps in the river
a seagull appears

for its war effort
a flag with a big E flies
above the tool and die works

the boys sneak
a quick look in the window
of a corset shop

Our shadows were longer now. The afternoon was wearing on and it must've been getting close to 5 o'clock. We had to get our papers soon, so we moved a little faster: fighting a bit and then by common consent moving down the street several yards. Cooled off by the water fountain and the fact that we each still had a long paper route to deliver, we eased up a bit. We were worn out by now and could barely swing our arms anyway.

a movie poster
with John Wayne fighting
a Japanese battalion

We finally got to the back of the newspaper office to pick up our evening papers. Through the roar of the presses and the shouts and bangings of the dispatchers, we managed to settle our differences. Arthur said, well, he thought he was satisfied and that he guessed I knew now not to say anything bad about his girl. I, choking a little, said, well, I guess she must be a pretty great girl to deserve such a fight in her honor, and I didn't intend to say anything about her again.

We were both a bit puffed up, not only physically from our cuts and bruises, but mentally and emotionally from the realization that we'd been in the longest fight the town had ever seen and that we'd both been cheered by the heroes of World War II. I don't remember if we actually shook hands, but he wasn't mad anymore, and the fight was really over. We got our papers and went our separate ways to deliver them.

the evening paper
on the darkening lawn
first star

A Boy's Holidays

The Holidays

We boys thought days that were called "holidays" should be days that got us out of school. It didn't always work that way. Easter fell on a Sunday and Valentine's Day and Halloween were not school holidays. A holiday that came during summer vacation had to be very special to get our attention. The Fourth of July was just the ticket. Spectacle, noise, parades, danger—it had everything a boy needed to get the summer off to a good start.

> it doesn't go off
> the kids dare each other
> to look under the tin can

For me as a boy there were seven holidays that were important for reasons above and beyond being days off from school: Valentine's Day, Easter, Memorial Day, The Fourth of July, Halloween, Thanksgiving, and Christmas. The last, however, with its two whole weeks of vacation, its presents and pageantry, was easily the biggest holiday of the year.

The special appeal to a boy of these seven days could be illustrated by the following images: a greeting card showing two red hearts with an arrow through them, a straw basket filled with jellybeans and a chocolate rabbit, a parade with flags swirling and bands playing, exploding firecrackers, a jack-o-lantern, a turkey chasing a football, and finally a Christmas tree surrounded by presents.

The rest of the year's holidays had little special meaning for boys unless they were—Hurray!—days off from school. Days when you could play baseball or basketball, or just wander in the woods, or along a railroad track, or read comic books. There were two of these days off in February, the same month as Valentine's Day. They were the Presidents' Birthdays: Washington's and Lincoln's.

Our teachers hoped these two holidays might mean more to us than just the chance to get out of school. They looked on Washington's Birthday as an occasion for impressing on us boys (and girls) the importance of being honest. Just before the actual day, the teacher would tell us in elaborate detail the story of young George Washington and the cherry tree. How, after he cut it down with his little hatchet, he "could not tell a lie" and so confessed to his father. Because he told the truth and was prepared to take his punishment, his father forgave him.

We also got the traditional stories of his boat ride across the Delaware through floes of ice, with the picture of him standing in the bow, the Star Spangled Banner starting to unfurl behind him, his praying for victory while on his knees in the snow at Valley Forge, the Father of Our Country, and so on. However in the earliest grades, the story of the poor cherry tree and George's honesty was the main feature.

> "who threw that paper plane?"
> all the boys look at the ceiling
> as if it came from there

For Abraham Lincoln's Birthday we had lessons on the value of lifting oneself up "by one's own bootstraps" and the importance of getting an education whatever the cost in effort and hard work. We heard the old stories about being born in a log cabin, studying by the light of the fireplace, splitting rails and walking behind a plow, on up to saving the Union, freeing the slaves, and preserving liberty and justice for all. With him we resolved "that government of the people, by the people, for the people, shall not perish from the earth."

> Civil War monument
> Old Glory flaps in the storm
> above a snow-covered cannon

However when we got down to what we liked about these holidays: they were two days *out* of school, *off* from school, *away* from school—HURRAAAY!!!

Perhaps the least liked holiday of the year was Labor Day, which marked the end of summer and put us on notice to be ready for the start of school. Its very name was ominous, reminding us that play was almost over and that the combined labor of classroom and homework was about to begin.

New Year's Day was a day when you were supposed to take stock of what you had accomplished in the past and determine to do better during the coming year.

> New Year's Day
> resolving to run a mile
> each morning

> New Year's Day
> resolving to do my homework
> —at least sometimes

> New Year's Day
> my mother suggests I resolve
> to keep my room cleaned-up

New Year's resolutions
my father orders that I resolve
to shovel the driveway NOW

So, I don't remember New Year's Day (or Eve) being a "big deal" with me or the boys I knew. Not only was it too close to Christmas, it was primarily a holiday for grown-ups. It was just another day during Christmas Vacation and only served to warn us, as Labor Day had earlier, that it was getting close to the time to go back to school again. There was nothing "new" about the weather. We were still in the middle of winter with its heavy snows and freezing winds. The new year would only really begin when the weather warmed-up enough in the spring for us to get out a baseball and gloves for the first game of catch.

lingering snow
the game of catch continues
into evening

Valentine's Day

Valentine's Day represented one of the important emotional conflicts that coursed through, or stumbled around in, a boy's heart. Since first recognizing that there was another sex, a boy's feelings swung from being attracted to, to feeling indifferent to, to actively disliking that sex's most immediate representatives: girls. These mixed feelings were easily shifted to Valentine's Day since the day and its events were all about love between boys and girls—a love that was symbolized by Cupid shooting an arrow into someone's heart, obviously a painful experience.

> picking up a book
> for the girl next to him
> the boy gets razzed

One year a boy might find himself feeling the joy of "being in love" and go to elaborate lengths to get just the right decorated-with-hearts-and-flowers card for that cute little girl with the braids in the third row. Another year he might dismiss the holiday with a sneering "Girls . . . yuk! Who cares about that sissy love stuff, anyway?" Put down or celebrated, it had, especially in his teen-age years, an important effect on the life and feelings of a boy.

In our New England classrooms, one of the earliest signs that spring was on its way was the warm red of Valentine hearts. Heavy drifts of snow kept the whole town and even the schoolyard locked in the cold of winter, but in the fourth grade at Sawyer School we were busy cutting out and hanging red and white paper hearts, many with lacework borders, all around the classroom.

We hung them on the walls and windows and even set them dangling from the long red and white streamers, ribbons, and banners we strung from wall to wall and across to the chains holding up the large white light-globes hanging from the ceiling. So hearts were flying all over the room.

Downtown, along Central Avenue, our main street, shop windows were exploding with red decorations. They stood out against the high banks of white snow that had been piled up by the snowplows along both sides of the street. Woolworth's plate-glass windows and those of Ora's Candy Shoppe were especially dazzling. Decorated with ornately tied red-ribbon bows and fancy cards and great heart-shaped boxes of candy—embossed in red and gold with elaborate curlicued letters and flowers—these displays sent a visual warmth through their windows and out onto the freezing sidewalks and street. People walking or even driving by could look through the still falling snow at the most red they'd seen since Christmas.

snowy Valentine's Day
my sister and two friends form
a Van Johnson fan club

the boy buys his dog
a comic valentine that says
"You dog you!"

no valentine card
the boy plays extra hard
on the basketball court

Valentine's Day
after school the boys have
a snowball fight

he throws a snowball
at the girl he has a crush on
— but softly

Sometimes we would have a thaw in February and by the 14th we might see bright sunlight glaring from the snow and hear the trickling sounds of meltwater from under large drifts or beneath the snowbanks left by plows and shovels. As the water gathered into larger streams it flowed gurgling along the curb's edge—sometimes hidden under snow, sometimes flashing in the sunlight—down to the corner drain where the sounds increased to a splashing ring and a whooshing whisperroaring echo. It was an audible as well as visual herald of things to come. For we knew that spring and baseball—and summer vacation—were not too far around that water-tumbling corner, even though the next day might bring the worst blizzard of the winter.

February snowstorm
putting off my homework
to oil my glove again

But an early thaw was the exception. Usually on Saint Valentine's Day we were issued the standard weather report for a February day in New Hampshire: freezing temperatures with ice, snow, and howling winds. In fact, February often was the severest month of the winter, which is probably why our ancestors made sure it was also the shortest.

winter wind
carving a heart in the beech tree
its few leaves rattle

So this Valentine's Day in the fourth grade we had a terrific snowstorm. But it started to get *really* bad too late in the morning to have school cancelled. If the weather was bad enough to call off school, they sounded the loud booming horn that the town used for fires or to sound the noon "whistle." When there was a big fire, and you knew the signal codes, you could tell by the number and length of the horn's blasts which part of town the fire was in. The signal for "no school" was something like one long and three short blasts. On a snowy morning we would hope to hear that "no school" signal right up to the last minute.

the yellow bus
appears out of the snowstorm
the boys groan

falling snow
covers a few snowballs
left in the snow fort

While the wind whirled sleet and snow against the big windows of our classroom, all the big globes were blazing with light from the ceiling, lighting up our decorations of colored paper, lace, and ribbons. And all around us, brightening up the room, were the cutout hearts, all different sizes, pasted on walls, windows, and blackboards. The ones on the windows were right up against the swirling, whispering, and wailing rattle of the storm. In great wind-driven waves, the snow and ice particles dashed against the bright red silhouettes.

We would have a party to exchange Valentine cards. We made a lot of them ourselves right in class, but some of us would also buy cards to give each other. They weren't exchanged directly in the classroom, that is not the ones for the party. They had to be addressed with the name of the recipient and then they went into a box to be handed out by the teacher later. She made sure everyone got at least one card. There were lots of comic cards put in the big box with the slot in top. When they were passed out later and opened, the addressee might find them signed "anonymous" or "from your father's moustache." These could contain some cruel comments or messages. But many of the romantic cards were also sent anonymously: signed "Your Secret Lover" or "An Admirer." Very few of us got the "Please be My Valentine" kind of card signed by the one we most hoped to get one from. And there was a lot of pretending we didn't care.

opening the valentine
the boy's face turns as red
as the card

Besides the cards we all got a handful of those tiny pastel-colored candy hearts with a short, sweet message on each one: "BE MINE," "KISS ME," "FOR EVER," I'M YOURS," "MY HEART," and "I LOVE YOU." There were also candy kisses, swirly cone-shaped drops of sweet milk chocolate each wrapped in crinkling tinfoil. And someone might even bring in a large chocolate heart, to break up and pass around. The big red or gold heart-shaped boxes of chocolates were too expensive for us kids, but sometimes the teacher would get one from an admirer and share it with us. The cover was often embossed with a golden Cupid shooting an arrow into a red heart.

slipping a candy heart
on her desk as he passes
back to his seat

Many of the cards, especially the ones from the teacher—which might be signed with just "Your Friend"—simply wished the person who got it a "Happy Valentine's Day," and that was a big part of what the whole occasion was about. To have a good time and be friendly. We could imagine what real romance might be like and think about having nice thoughts about the opposite sex, even having a real "sweetheart," whatever that was, but except for that strange ache when we looked at the cute girl with the golden braids, we boys usually associated love with those boring few minutes at the end of a Tim McCoy western when he said goodbye to the rancher's pretty daughter—then rode off into the sunset.

We approved of his riding off, probably towards another exciting adventure, and champed at the bit until he got away. We were relieved when the girl sometimes kissed the horse and spared the cowboy.

We would never fall in love, unless it happened years later, say in the seventh or eighth grade, when we might fall on our head and lose our mind. Girls, we imagined, had more immediate concerns with the idea of romantic love. After all they were girls.

> the tomboy
> tears up a valentine
> from the class clown

Our fourth-grade teacher, Miss Bullard, was a modern day romantic. She let us sing big-band popular hits, such as Jimmy Dorsey's "Amapola." She would bring in a record player and we could sing right along wih Helen O'Connell and Bob Eberly. The boys liked the big-band jazz sound but didn't take the romantic lyrics seriously. We either didn't sing or just hummed when we came to such gooey phrases as "my pretty little poppy" and "so sweet and heavenly."

> after the party
> changing the initials in the heart
> carved on my desk

What many of us got out of the celebration, I think, was that while still in the grip of our long northern winter, we could have the bright and warm red relief of Valentine's Day to quicken our pulse and send us a message that the ice and snow would soon be gone. Even if you were disappointed that the golden braids seemed oblivious to your existence, the troubled yearning she stirred in you was a live and intense feeling. A sad warmth that enclosed a beating hope for the future. Someday she would know what a wonderful person you are—you would forgive her for her coolness and you would both live happily ever after. But you would never tell anyone that. Except maybe your dog, who could be trusted not to repeat it.

> on the way home
> reading the valentine again
> steady snowfall

Easter

We considered Easter a holiday for small children or for "religious" people and not something of much interest to us older boys of ten and eleven or more. Grown-ups might go to church and feel uplifted by the thought of the resurrection of Christ and how his blood and body shared at communion would someday bring them into the glory of Heaven, but if our parents did manage to shepherd us into church on Easter Sunday we just sat and fidgeted through the sermon and thought of that new baseball glove in the window of Seavey's Combination Hardware and Sporting Goods Store. Or we looked at the stained glass windows to see if the sun had come out yet so there'd be good weather for the sandlot game that afternoon.

> bells on Easter Sunday
> a robin on the church lawn
> cocks its head
>
> getting dressed for church
> the kid puts on his cowboy shirt
> and Sheriff's badge

during the sermon
the boy squeezes a rubber ball
to improve his swing

When we were in the fifth or sixth grade, we could still remember
when Easter was a BIG deal. That was way back when we were little
kids in the first, second, or even third grade. We went to Sunday school
back in those days, learned about the Golden Rule, and felt close to
Jesus, sorry for His suffering and thankful that He had sacrificed himself
for us. We knew the story of the rock being rolled aside from the cave
and His rising from the dead. And we knew that though this miracle
happened almost two thousand years ago, it still meant something
important for us today and could affect us in wondrous ways for all
time—and even beyond time.

"Onward Christian Soldiers"
the boy tries to sing bass
but keeps slipping up

I'm afraid most boys, even when they were little, found more immediate
joys of a material nature at Easter, and the long-range spiritual ones were
only vague shadows that floated just out of sight above the candles on the

altar. Easter was exciting when we were little kids not because Christ was risen and going to save our souls, but because the Easter Bunny was going to come "hopping down the bunny trail" with a basket full of goodies.

We would get straw baskets lined with shiny green cellophane grass and filled with colored eggs, jellybeans, chocolate rabbits, and various other candies. The jellybeans came in red, blue and purple, green, orange, yellow, white, and black. I would always look for the licorice-tasting black ones.

There were even chocolate rabbits as large as real ones, much too big to get in our baskets. I saw one that big in a store window once and a kid in our class swore he actually ate one of them. Whatever the size, you broke these brown cottontails into chunks of sweetness that melted slowly in your mouth. The taste of candy wonders and the bright colors of flowers and painted eggs and the storybook thoughts of magical rabbits bringing us presents all made Easter a day for celebration. If it was warm enough, there would be lawn parties with ice cream and cake and party favors that you pulled apart with a loud "SNAP" so a small toy would pop out. And there would be an Easter-egg hunt with a prize for the kid who found the most colored eggs hidden around the yard.

> Easter morning
> dew on a cellophane wrapper
> in the driveway

in the grass
a soft rain is washing
an Easter egg

Easter afternoon
not a crumb remains
of the chocolate rabbit

Even the ritual of coloring the eggs the day before, on newspapers spread on the kitchen table, was more fun than the ceremonies at church on Easter day. Using a special egg-coloring kit, you dipped a hard-boiled egg into a mixture of water and dye to cover it all over with a solid pastel hue. Or you dipped part of the egg in one color and swirled the other part in a different color.

Or we got out our watercolors and a small paint brush. Then mixed the colors in the little pockets of the egg carton to make different shades of blues and reds and yellows. We tried all kinds of designs on those hard-boiled eggs: spotting them, striping them, whirling blue lines in and out of red circles, splashing yellow suns next to green stars. Dots and streaks got all over our hands, and the spring sun danced through the Saturday afternoon kitchen window to throw bright shadows around our artwork.

while coloring
the Easter eggs
reading the comics

climbing the apple tree
white petals almost hide
the robins' blue eggs

As we got older, Easter Sunday continued to be the most important day of the year for going to church, so we went along with our families, dragging our feet. Though we might not have gone much or at all the rest of the year, it was assumed you would go at Easter and you knew it would do absolutely no good to fight it.

Still, Easter had acquired a new meaning for us boys. It was a sign that the long winter was ending—and that the weather was going to get better and better for baseball. It was also a sign that the school year would soon be over. If Easter's here, can summer vacation be far away? NO!

So we hoped it would be a sunny spring day with the field finally dried out enough for a real baseball game. We figured girls probably liked to go to church. They could show off their new Easter dresses—and hats—and shoes. We wanted to get out in the sunlight and play ball.

Puddles or not! Yet even after sitting through church, we often had to go home for dinner before we could get away.

> outside the church
> the silence of the parked cars
> in the morning sunlight

> end of the service
> the minister suddenly appears
> by the door

After Sunday dinner there would hopefully be enough afternoon sun left to get a game going. If there weren't visiting friends or relatives. If there were, we might have to be polite and keep them company, especially if they had brought their kids. We might even have to line up on the front lawn for a group picture in our Sunday clothes. The ladies would tilt their Easter bonnets and smile and say "cheese" at the little Brownie box-camera.

> squinting at the sun
> the kid holds his toy sailboat
> for the family picture

after Easter dinner
the boy has to play with cousin Emily
missing the game

a secret reward:
playing doctor with
the pretty cousin

Meanwhile, back there in church, you hoped none of these things would happen (except the last, which you couldn't foresee) and that you would soon be throwing a baseball. You passed the time watching the sun filter through the stained glass windows, lighting them up as it passed through them. Turning your head you could see the light carrying the rich patterns of blues and golds, reds and greens through the air and spreading colored shadows throughout the congregation.

And then you might notice the Easter hats, worn by the girls and ladies, flowering all over the church. They seemed to be trying to outdo the elaborate floral arrangements around the altar. The latter were always dominated by the white bells and the long stems of the Easter lilies. The singing was more spirited and the minister spoke more enthusiastically than at any other time of the year except Christmas. Reverend Huffer's voice rose dramatically as he approached the rolled-back stone of the tomb to gaze with wonder with Mary at the empty shroud. As he went on about what this momentous event meant to our immortal souls my mind would drift away . . .

. . . to wander back outside, where the vacant lot was drying out in the sunshine and just waiting to become a baseball diamond. Later that day I would stand at the plate and line a drive right out to where the going sun would begin to touch down towards the tops of the trees.

biking to the field
under a cloudless sky
my glove on the handlebars

throw to first
the ball follows its shadow
into the sunlit mitt

shagging the fly ball
I step on an Easter egg
hidden in the grass

Memorial Day

To many grown-ups, Memorial Day was the beginning of summer. Not to us kids. We still had two or three more weeks of school. We did get the day off, though, and there would be a big parade. We boys loved a parade and parades were especially important during World War II. Many of our games in those days involved pretending to be soldiers fighting the Nazis, or sailors on a battleship in the Pacific, or pilots in a dogfight with Japanese Zeros. So it was a thrill to see our heroes marching right down Central Avenue. A few times I even got to be in the parade with them. In my Boy Scout uniform I marched at the head of my troop carrying the American flag.

The parade would have long ranks of marching soldiers, marines and sailors. At some point a company of soldiers would halt in place and do the manual of arms with their rifles, their abrupt, synchronized movements punctuated with sharp slaps and clicks as the rifles sprang into new positions or the bolts were snapped back.

The National Guard had several jeeps and trucks pulling artillery pieces, large cannons that swung menacingly around when the parade turned a corner. All the equipment was polished and shining, the uniforms trim and neat. Once there was a platoon of Airborne Commandos whose boots glittered like knives in the morning sunlight.

And there were all kinds of bands: military bands from the nearby naval and air bases, the High School band, and the bands of various civic organizations. In the early days there were mounted troops and the horses would do different kinds of steps: high-stepping, prancing, or a slow trot.

misty rain
confetti sticks to the hoofs
of the parading horses

The parade would end up at the town's biggest and oldest cemetery on the Dover Point Road, where prayers and speeches were given in praise of those who had died for freedom in all our wars and somebody would always recite Lincoln's Gettysburg Address. With their rifles pointing at the sky, squads of soldiers would fire salutes to the war dead, and then taps would sound sad and long under the blue May sky, stretching over the wide lawns of the cemetery, and fading into the surrounding pine trees. The crowd would slowly disperse, some people staying to decorate the graves.

after the speeches
the honored dead return
to their silence

evening
in the deserted cemetery
bird song

In the 1940's, Memorial Day had a very immediate and special meaning. During the war, our friends and relatives were fighting and dying for us. In the years after the war, as veterans returned and marched in the parade and we realized that thousands more would never return, the day took on a greater poignancy. There were special observances on the radio. The president would speak. And we would hear a description of the laying of the wreath on the tomb of the Unknown Soldier.

Memorial Day was originally established to honor those who served in the Civil War, Armistice Day for those who were in the First World War, and Independence Day, or the Fourth of July, was about the Revolutionary War. But on each of these holidays we were supposed to remember everyone who had fought or was fighting for our country and freedom, in whatever conflict, and we always had a parade to honor them. All the parades we had in those years blend into one big parade in my memory.

We had several ways of showing our appreciation for what America's servicemen and women were doing to preserve our way of life in the war against the Axis. Parades, war-bond rallies, and other demonstrations of support were constantly taking place. I went with the Boy Scouts on the back of a truck collecting used papers and magazines and scrap metal for the war effort. Kids bought war stamps at school, collecting them into booklets that when filled would get them a war bond. We also sold stamps and bonds door to door in our neighborhoods during "Bond Drives". When the war ended in the summer of 1945, I was fourteen years old and had just recently graduated from the eighth grade at Sawyer School.

I remember the day the war ended. It was a hot day and I was working at a summer job shoveling sandy gravel onto a big screen. Screening out the rocks in order to get sand to make a cement walk. With my shirt off and sweating in the sun, I was into the rhythm of shoveling. I could at times really get into a simple physical job like that, enjoying the repetition. My muscles would work smoothly over and over again like parts of a machine. Even the hot sun seemed to be a part of what I was doing. My body was deep into it with my mind miles away when I was startled from my concentration by the noise of car horns blowing and honking from the nearby highway. Then I heard repeated blasts from the distant town's noon whistle, but I knew it wasn't noon. I dropped my shovel and ran towards the road. People were shouting out their car windows: "The War is over!" and "The Japs have surrendered!"

summer day in Dover
the World War ends with
a honking of horns

The Fourth of July

We started to get the fireworks for the Fourth of July a week or two ahead of time: fireworks and sparklers—and rolls of caps for our cap guns. These guns were usually modeled after a cowboy's pearl-handled six-shooter, but sometimes they were in the square shape of a detective's black automatic. We would be busy banging caps on the sidewalk with a rock if we didn't have our cap guns with us. We also threw marble-sized "torpedoes" onto the pavement, where they exploded on impact.

We had large double packets of small firecrackers all tied together. Each individual "cracker" was about as long as a wooden match and a little bit thinner than a pencil. You would take one off the packet and light it while holding it in your hand, then fling it away so it exploded in the air, or at the feet of someone who'd just thrown one at you. Some packets had the fuses all tied together so you could light one end and throw the whole packet into the air and the crackers would explode in rapid succession, sounding like machine-gun fire.

The firecrackers were always colored fire-engine red. Some of the bigger ones and the exploding rockets had a blue and white design added to the red, in a star-spangled banner pattern. A lot of them came in packages wrapped in bright yellow and red paper with Chinese characters written on them.

paper flowers
open slowly in a glass of water
the Fourth booms outside

the firecracker doesn't go off
slowly creeping up on it
poking it with a stick

hearing it again
the story of the kid who
lost two fingers

Sometimes we broke open a firecracker, spilling the powder in a little pile on the ground. When lit with a match it sputtered and sparked and danced with light. We often had a slow burning stick of punk to use for lighting fuses—so we wouldn't have to keep striking matches. It smoldered like a stick of incense and added a ritualistic flavor to the fun. You blew on the end to knock off the ash and to make it glow before touching it to the fuse. Bigger crackers (like the four- and five-inchers) we put under tin cans to see the echoing explosions throw the cans high into the air.

> the tin can flies up
> the sound of the five-incher
> rings on and on

In the morning there would be a big patriotic parade down the main street of town. It was more festive than the Memorial Day parade, less solemn and stately. Usually we had two men and a boy recreate "The Spirit of '76": one guy with a bandage around his head playing the fife, an older fellow in the middle carrying the flag, and marching at his right the young drummer boy. They would be leading a small group of marchers dressed as Minutemen to remind us that the War for Independence was won by ordinary citizens who took up arms for freedom.

> Old Glory passes
> the boy scout salutes
> his dog's tail wags

Then came a contingent of soldiers from an army base in the next state. There were fifty or so sailors from the nearby seaport of Portsmouth, a few ranks of retired policemen and firemen back in uniform, one of the town's fire trucks, bands from the local men's lodges, a troop of boy scouts, some Scottish bagpipers, veterans' groups, and always some people on horses, among them one in a cowboy outfit and another wearing an Indian warbonnet.

But, by the time I got into high school, the biggest treat for me was to see the drum majorettes and the cheerleaders marching in front of the high school band.

> the baton twirlers
> spin a glitter of sunlight
> ahead of the band

I loved to hear the stirring Sousa marches while I watched those high-stepping beauties shake their short uniform skirts with each lift of their lovely long legs. Twirling their glittering batons and throwing them up into the bright blue July sky, catching them again with perfect precision, they looked like movie stars. Their soft, long hair, flowing lightly in the breeze, was shaken and set shimmering by their meticulously precise movements. There were two very special majorettes, one a blonde and one a brunette: Carolyn and Barbara. They brought a boy's most hidden fantasies right out into broad daylight, into real-life living color, marching right down the middle of Central Avenue. And behind them came the less regal, more instantly erotic, curving, flesh-flaring warm inviting jumping cartwheeling panty-glimmering leg flashing breast bouncing hair flying heart pounding cheerleaders in all their young vibrant vital boy-wounding glory.

And the band played on.

> the Drum Majorette winks
> at . . . the star fullback
> looming behind me

By the night of the Fourth itself, most of us would have shot off all of our fireworks. Then—this was when we were still pretty small—my father had his own display for the family and neighbors right on our front lawn. We waved sparklers around, delighting in the faintly hissing sparks of fire jumping around us like small shooting stars. They created a little wavering ring of light in the surrounding night.

My father, after making sure everyone was a safe distance away, would set off a series of loud booming firecrackers. Then Catherine Wheels, which whirled across the night sky in great spiralling galaxies. Finally, the sky-rockets. These were attached to sticks that you stuck into the ground. They streaked high up towards the stars and flared out into bright red and yellow fountains of light.

When I got older there were professional fireworks in the park or at the beach and we went to these instead, and so my father retired from show business. Now the heavens lit up with great extravaganzas of colored lights, flares, streamers, bursts, and spangling, glittering, shimmering panoramas of spectacular pyrotechnics. Coloring the passing clouds, these displays would explode across the whole sky, showering outwards in great circles, and then fall slowly towards the earth as they went out.

They produced a thrilling barrage of sounds: from the screams of rockets to big bomb-like booms, with all sorts of whistling, sputtering, fizzing, banging, and thundering in between. Sometimes a great whooshing sound would rise up into the blackness—and suddenly streaming lines of light would appear out of nowhere high above us. As they started to arc over they would explode at their tips into large starbursts, and falling from out of these were phosphorous-blue electric-like sparks and streaks that seemed to wink on and off as they spun through the night sky and then the big BANG would thud back to earth just as the silent explosion of lights started to fade.

> fireworks crowd
> Aaahhh for the lights
> Oooohh for the boom

After the last, great crescendos of light and noise had marked the finale—a huge American flag, made up of red, white, and blue fireworks flaring all at once, rippling Old Glory's stars and stripes across the night sky—the crowd broke up and we would walk slowly home, or to our car, the sky suddenly dark and dull, wisps of smoke from the fireworks still drifting earthward.

By the time we got to the car or out of the park, we would notice that there were far greater fires up there, far beyond where the fireworks had been exploding. The stars in the Milky Way drifted like a river of lights across the vastness of the night sky and my eye and mind flowed with and then beyond them to even more distant stars, going deeper and deeper into the endlessness of space until the darkness and its lights seemed to go on forever.

Fourth of July milkshake
the soda-fountain lights flare
in its vanishing bubbles

after the fireworks
all the headlights come on
in the parking lot

dark road
sparks from a cigarette
bounce behind a car

low on the horizon
a distant fireworks display
high above: the moon

Halloween

Hollowing out the pumpkin. We would sit around the kitchen table and start by cutting out a lid from the top. You used a large pumpkin with a solid stem still attached as a handle for the lid. After a lot of cutting, scraping, and scooping, at last it was hollowed out, with a fairly smooth, circular wall inside to make a pale, light-colored interior. The outside was a deep orange with vertical seams curving to the top. Now you could cut out the face. Should it smile or frown? Have some gapped teeth? Have triangles for eyes?

>the pumpkin grins
>at its own insides filling
>the bowl

Somehow a big, grinning smile seemed more eerie than a frown. The eyes were triangles. The nose, a more vertical triangle. When the jack-o-lanterns were done, candles were inserted and lit, and the kitchen light was put out.

Three disembodied faces sat glowing on the kitchen table. Two grinning insanely (mine and my kid sister's), and one sadly frowning (our little brother's). The smells of candle wax and warming pumpkin scented the air.

I took mine outside into the autumn night and placed it on the wooden picnic table under the pitch pines at the edge of the side lawn. The wind rustled the pines. The stars in the Milky Way seemed to be blowing across the cold sky. I turned the grinning face toward the house.

> windy night
> the moon flying behind clouds
> glows through the gaps

The pumpkin head seemed to possess a spirit that the light brought to life. A light broken into four pieces: two eyes, a nose, and a mouth. Through these holes you could see behind the face into a little room all lit up—glowing like an enchanted room in a story from the Arabian Nights.

> an owl hoots
> the candle flame flutters
> in the carved pumpkin

After I went back inside, we all looked out the window from the darkness of the house at the jack-o-lantern. In the blackness beneath the trees, in the surrounding starlit darkness of the whole night, it glittered there like a visitor from another world.

And then the wind suddenly blew the candle out. And the face was gone into the darkness.

> Halloween
> three small ghosts with jack-o-lanterns
> hurry past the cemetery

A few Halloweens there was actually a party, with refreshments and games, and with decorations from the 5 & 10 cent store: paper cutouts of black cats, and bats, and witches on broomsticks. There were big bowls of kernel-corn candy—orange and yellow candies shaped like kernels of corn—and sticks of black licorice. Orange and black were the colors of Halloween. Streamers of orange and black crinkly crepe paper were strung about the rooms and real carved pumpkins glittered on the mantel of the fireplace at this party in the house of a girl from our seventh-grade class. And there were also several fake "carved" pumpkins scattered about. Made of some kind of composition, a fore-runner of plastic, these added to the festive air as they too had candles, but they were dead, static containers compared to the glowing presences of the real pumpkins.

> the grinning pumpkin
> its pool of light flickers
> on the porch steps

Everyone was in costumes and masks or false-faces. There was a witch, a ghost, a pirate, Little Bo-Peep, a sailor, Cinderella, a big-toothed monster, and even a Saint Bernard dog with a small keg around his neck. We played games like pin-the-tail on the donkey, blindman's buff, bobbing for apples, and spin the bottle.

I was still shy of girls and my first real kiss was still years away. I avoided getting too close to the small circle of kids sitting on the floor around a Coke bottle lying on its side. They took turns spinning the bottle. If the person it pointed to when it came to rest was of the opposite sex, the "spinner" got to give her or him a kiss. If it pointed to someone of your own sex, you lost your turn.

> the bottle stops
> she hides her masked face
> in her hands

Her black mask only covered around her eyes so I knew who it was. She was pretty and soft and had long, glittering black locks. I didn't want to see her kiss anybody, so I walked out to the hall and sat down in a stairwell to wonder why I should feel so embarrassed when I had avoided even watching her get kissed and was now well away from the scene of the crime.

Getting up, I brushed by a dangling skeleton hanging in the hall. I had to get my mind on something else. A pretty girl was an enigmatic being who could set my heart pounding and get me all flushed and hot in the face just at the thought of having to speak to her, never mind kissing her. Though I might tingle with delight if I were alone at home and fantasizing about kissing her, I was a tongue-tied jerk if I actually encountered her face to face.

The game of spin-the-bottle was over and she was drinking a Coke when I went back into the living room where the party was centered. She had a smooth, silk-like dress on and was dressed as a princess with a little crown-tiara. I had on a cowboy's vest and chaps, and a gunbelt with a six-shooter in the holster. She had her mask off now and she looked over at me. Before she could say anything I fled like a zombie towards a group of boys who were poking each other and laughing, probably about something stupid.

> blindman's buff
> he listens for the rustle
> of her taffeta

Bobbing for apples in a big washtub was a good way to break the spell cast by a pretty girl. To wake you up, there was nothing quicker than splashing your head into a bunch of apples floating in a tub of cold water.

Unless there was a very small apple—which there never was—you had to drive the apple with your mouth to the bottom of the tub, submerging your head, in order to get enough pressure to drive your teeth into the firm skin of the bouncing red McIntosh and lift it, dripping, out of the tub. It was wet work, but it cooled off some of the fire fanned by the pretty princess, a fire which still glowed whenever I caught sight of her.

some apples still float
in the big round washtub
as the lights go out

All the lights except for those in the jack-o-lanterns were put out so that we could tell ghost stories. After that we talked to the dead through a Ouija board and some of the boys tried to scare the girls, and themselves, with moans, groans, and ghostly howls. So when it came time to leave, we all tried to have some company on the walk home.

Halloween party
as we walk home in the dark
a loon laughs on the pond

Then there were Halloweens when we were bad and rang doorbells—or stuck pins in them to keep them ringing—and ran away, rapped on windows, put rocks in mailboxes, howled in backyards, and maybe some of us even soaped a window or two, though I can't remember that I ever even wanted to do something that bad.

So we were pretty civilized along our part of the road and we usually just went up someone's walk in our ghostly sheets and knocked on the Indian-corn decorated front door, said "Trick or treat" and were handed an orange or some candy for our trick-or-treat bag.

Then we might wander up the dark country road who-whooing like an owl or moaning like a ghost until we came to the next house, where a pumpkin-headed figure stuffed with straw was propped up on the lawn. We walked under a large bat hanging from the dark porchlight, and then jumped three feet in the air when the door suddenly opened and a monster holding its own head under its arm shook a long (rubber) knife at us.

Halloween
the chimes ring deep in the house
but nobody comes

Thanksgiving

Thanksgiving was probably less a boy's holiday than most of our other favorites, except maybe for Easter (or Valentine's Day during those times you were against anything that had to do with girls). Because, though it was a holiday and we had off from school, you were still supposed to learn something.

The day before, our teacher would tell us we should realize how blessed we were and be thankful. And, she would go on, when we were enjoying our turkey and cranberry sauce on Thanksgiving Day we should remember the history that lay behind this holiday. Then she told the story of how the Pilgrims and Indians started the tradition of Thanksgiving. First the Indians helped the Pilgrims survive the harsh winters of New England. And later the Pilgrims invited the Indians to celebrate the autumn harvest by joining in a feast and giving thanks to God.

> pumpkin stand
> the evening sunlight shines
> on the Indian corn

But a boy could enjoy the festive atmosphere, the visiting relatives, the warmth and food, and the bubbly, unnaturally good-humored grown-ups sipping their wine or drinking their beer or tossing back their little shots of whiskey, and talking, talking, talking, and the men joking around, the grown women—mothers—suddenly shy and girlish.

And such things to eat: beginning with soups and salads and stalks of celery with olives and carrot sticks; moving on to the turkey & stuffing, cranberry sauce, mashed turnip and squash, potatoes with gravy, string beans, peas and carrots, and little onions; and ending with pumpkin and mince pies (or our favorite, lemon meringue), ice cream, fruits, nuts and candies. And big glasses of cold milk or soda (that we called tonic) to wash it all down. After we were stuffed, my younger sister, Agnes, and my little brother, Dickie, got to pull and break the turkey's wishbone, which had been drying in the kitchen.

> another helping
> father loosens his belt
> mother gets up and down
>
> breaking the wishbone
> my kid sister gets the big half
> silence for her secret wish

wearing turkey feathers
the kids do a war dance
around the dog

Thanksgiving was one of the few meals of the year when we said grace at the table. We would peek to see that everyone had their eyes closed. They all did, except for Uncle James who was taking another sip of his whiskey. It was usually a very simple prayer giving thanks for the food on the table. Or someone might recite the Lord's Prayer. Sometimes an older uncle would come up with a concise sermon:

Dear Lord,
Thank you for all your blessings. Please help us to make better use of them, to appreciate them more, and to be more worthy of them.

Amen.

What saved Thanksgiving and turned it into a real holiday for us boys was that it was the day of the last football game of the season. Every year at Thanksgiving, the Green Wave of Dover High School played against its traditional foe, the Clippers of Portsmouth—the seaport city downriver on the other side of the Piscataqua River. In Dover the game was played at Bellamy Park, and in the morning—so everyone could get home after the game and have Thanksgiving dinner early in the afternoon.

> the football field
> snow falls on the bleachers
> drifts in the end zones

The fourth Thursday in November was usually cold, sometimes rainy, sometimes snowy—and once in a while the game would be played in a sleety blizzard. It didn't matter. It was always a great game. The big game of the year. The colder and wetter it got the more warm and excited you felt. Up in the stands, surrounded by hundreds of other heavily bundled-up, enthusiastic spectators, you ran and twisted away from tacklers—in your imagination—along with the helmeted athletes down on the field. When you were on the Junior Varsity, you had scrimmaged against some of them, and had once helped to tackle the star fullback. Now you cheered them on.

> across the field
> the opposing stands blur
> in the snowstorm

freezing day
pulling my fingers into fists
inside my mittens

And somehow the girls, with only their flushed pretty faces showing and a few locks of hair escaping from under their warm woolen hats— the rest of their bodies in heavy coats with pulled-up collars, draped and swirled with long scarves—seemed even prettier and more desirable than usual, warm and cuddly looking, under their hoods or umbrellas.

There's the girl I've had a crush on since the eighth grade. Her dark curls frame her pink cheeks and a few snowflakes are rainbowing in her long dark eyelashes. But her bright eyes are searching for her boyfriend out on the field, a starter on Dover's football squad.

In spite of the ache of not having your love returned, you have a warm feeling just seeing her, just being part of the same crowd, rooting for the same team. The freezing rain and sleet and the cold winds only make us feel more awake and alive. We roar our support and send the Green Wave of Dover juggernauting its way out onto the field.

freezing rain
cheering the football team
and waving a soggy pennant

the hot-dog stand's steam
rises into the falling snow
a roar from the crowd

Even the red hot dog in its golden-brown bun, the stripe of yellow mustard down its middle, and the white paper napkin keeping it warm, was a delightful combination to hold, look at, and eat (not the napkin) in that freezing, grey November weather. Many people brought thermos bottles of hot soup or coffee. Some of the older folks had much stronger cheer in theirs.

As the teams lined up for the kickoff, the cheerleaders, wearing hooded jackets, but still bare-legged, ran into a line facing us and started doing high jumps and high kicks and waving their arms and punching the sky, urging us on to even louder cheering, spelling out D-O-V-E-R GO, GO, GO, GO! GO-O-O-O DOVER!

Our heroes ploughed through the turf and mud and slush, pushing further and further into the enemies' territory and in the stands we stood and swayed and roared our approval. Now from 20 yards out "Mr. Inside," Dick Jennison, surprises the opposing line, drops back and throws that wet, slippery football through the driving sheets of sleet deeeep into the end zone where lanky Peter Bourque jumps high, reaches up with his big hands and pulls the spinning ball out of the whirling snow and wraps himself around it as he falls back to earth, amidst a crush of dripping, mud-splattered players from both sides.

> waking in the snowy mud
> the left tackle finds his face
> in a puddle

And now we and the cheerleaders go into a frenzy of heated— HOT—celebration for our team as the place-kick for extra point raises the football into the wind where it disappears into the mist and sleet right between the goalposts.

> end run
> the storm holds back the runner
> for our tacklers

We all dig in and then drive back the dogged tribe from down the river to hold them scoreless. Dover wins the big game 7-0. As we head for our cars or for the hike, or hitchhike, home through the storm, our thoughts go ahead of us to the tables loaded with food that our mothers have been preparing all morning. And all we have to do the rest of the day is stuff ourselves, and after the relatives leave, just lie around reading comic

books or listening to the radio and here it is still only Thursday and there
is no school until next Monday!

> after the football game
> falling snow slowly covers
> the scarred field

Christmas

Where I grew up in Maine and New Hampshire, Christmas was always cold and white, and sometimes it was snowing on Christmas Eve. We would already have from six inches to several feet of snow covering the ground, and a snowman, with pieces of coal for eyes, was standing sentinel in the front yard to welcome Santa Claus.

> fading into drifts
> the snowman slowly disappears
> in the storm

After a heavy snowfall the world was filled with a strange quietness and sounds traveled through the air with a strange echo or soft ringing around them. When I was three or four years old there were still some horse-drawn sleighs (in a neighborhood called The Half-Way, between Old Orchard and Saco, Maine) and the quiet, greeting-card snowscapes lasted a while longer than in later years when snowplows would lose little time in rumbling through the stillness to plow them away.

In those older days the snow was packed on the roads by horses pulling heavy rollers, so the sleighs could slide swiftly over it. The sound of the jingling bells on the horse's harness floated across a landscape hushed by the deep snow and freezing cold, while sprays of snowflakes flew up at the end of the sleigh's runners to flash in the icy sunlight.

> the stillness
> within the falling snow
> far off sleigh bells

The Christmas tree, a balsam fir, would be standing in the living room all spangled with decorations and lights and sending a woodsy fragrance through the house. It would be near a window so the lights could shine out at night and passersby could also enjoy the glowing colors.

> the little girl
> hangs all the ornaments
> on the nearest branch

Draped in great swirls of tinsel that looked like icicles and drifts of snow, the six- or seven-foot tree was hung with different-sized balls and figures of delicate glass shell. The shiny colored balls were globe or oval-shaped and reflected everything around them. When they occasionally fell and broke, they shivered into slivers and shards, the insides looking like pieces of curved, silvered mirrors.

The glass figures were angels and Santa Clauses, or reindeer pulling a tiny sleigh, or maybe a miniature snow-covered Christmas tree hanging on the real tree. And there were always some red and white striped candy canes hooked on the branches along with a few red-net stockings holding various kinds of hard Christmas candies.

And on the very top of the tree an angel with outstretched wings hovered protectively and promisingly over our world.

The strings of painted lights glowed serenely through the night. We didn't get blinking lights until sometime after World War II. The old lights after a few years of use would get scratches in the color that covered them so that streaks of the yellow-white light inside would gleam through the red or blue or green colored bulbs that were shaped like candle flames.

getting home late
through falling snow
the Christmas lights in our window

leaning on the telephone-pole
I climb over a plowed snowbank
to get into our driveway

opening the storm door
it makes a smooth arc in the snow
on the back porch

I remember one year we went to a Christmas party in an upstairs hall of a building in downtown Saco. I received a red-net Christmas stocking full of hard candies and an orange, an apple, a small striped candy cane, and a tiny toy boat. I had lined up for it along with about fifteen or twenty kids waiting our turns for a stuffed stocking from a red-suited, ho-ho'ing Santa Claus, who picked up the stockings from under a huge lit Christmas tree. The toys were varied so a girl would get a tiny doll or a game of ball-and-jacks. A boy might get a yo-yo or a toy soldier.

This party—one of my earliest memories—was at a Scots' lodge. My mother, born and raised in Glasgow, Scotland, kept in touch through the lodge with the other Scotswomen in our area. Before the handing out of the stockings by Santa Claus (who, I learned years later, was played by my mother's Aunt Agnes) there was some entertainment. Various members and their children sang or danced, recited a poem or played a musical instrument. My mother sang the Scottish song "Sweet Afton" and the Christmas hymn "O Little Town of Bethlehem." I was about three or four years old and I recited "Twinkle, Twinkle, Little Star," to the accompaniment of an old upright piano, which had a lonely, echoing "tinkle, twinkle" sound.

> in the drafty hall
> the sound of an upright piano
> playing Christmas carols

That is the only Christmas celebration at the lodge I remember. Though it is a fond and early recollection and stands out in bright colors and second-story auditorium sounds of a plinkety-plunking piano and a variety of singing voices, including my own childish pipings, the Christmas memories that are the brightest and most achingly immediate to me to the present day are those that I experienced at home. They merge together from different homes we had in the early 1930's to the mid 1940's with here and there a particular incident or image standing out in front of the general picture, but all coming together to make "my Christmas."

The same angel with outstretched wings stood on top of all our Christmas trees through those years. Though I think it was finally

replaced by a star after the war. In those later years, when I was in high
school, the magic glow diminished a bit and the cynical teen-ager lost
some of his sense of wonder at the sight of Christmas lights shining on
a tree. But he could still get pretty excited at seeing the presents spread
around it, whether they were wrapped in Christmas paper or just in their
bright and shiny newness.

> opening the gift
> the wrapping paper rustles
> as I take a breath

But the Christmases before disillusion began to tarnish things seem to
flow together into one grand Christmas that was repeated like a ringing
of bells echoing down through the years, fading and then being renewed
again in the frozen depths of each winter.

The major presents might change with each year. The toy soldiers.
The sled with the gleaming varnished wood surface and the flying
runners. The red wagon with the wood-slatted detachable sides. And the
elaborate Lionel train-set with all the curved and straight pieces of track
to put together, with the train station, and the little gates to lower at the
crossing, and with all the different train cars: the steam engine, the coal
car, passenger cars, boxcars, a tankcar, a flatcar, and the caboose.

the toy train
comes around a bend
shadows in a boxcar

One year there was the little milk wagon pulled by a little horse, with tiny wooden milkbottles in a tiny metal carrying-rack. Another, a cowboy belt spread out under the Christmas tree with two pearl-handled six-shooters in the holsters. Later there was the pair of skis standing behind the tree and reflecting back from their shiny wood the many colored lights that now blinked as well as glowed.

And always the two or three books. Always in the early years, these were westerns. And usually wrapped only in their luminously painted book-jackets. The picture of a cowboy with a six-shooter in his hand, wearing a yellow shirt and leather chaps, leading his reddish-brown horse down into a bluegrey craggy canyon, his white ten-gallon hat shading his face, while, above, an Indian with an Apache blue headband peers over the edge of an overhanging sunlit cliff—the colors of shadows and sunlight zigzagging across the cover—had more sparkle and magic than any gold-dusted, striped or snowmanned, or red-suited-santa-claus decorated wrapping paper, with all its elaborate ribbons and bows, could ever have. Especially when you saw it under a branch of the Christmas tree, where it was turned into a lurid lobby-poster by the blue, yellow, red, and green lights.

reading the western
a breeze along the trail
lifts my horse's mane

reading the western
I stand in my stirrups
to see the cloud of dust

reading the western
the sound of pots and pans
from the kitchen

Yes. Christmas was presents. When the world rewarded you just for being there. Oh, we were supposed to be good, to deserve all this, but we knew we weren't as good as we should have been—and we still got them. Our father would tell us the story of a certain Christmas when he was a boy in Holland. That year he had been oh, so, not so good—well, bad! For not paying enough attention in school or to his chores, he'd gotten only a piece of coal in his wooden shoe.

But his stern old Saint Nicholas couldn't have been the kind and jolly Santa Claus who took such great care of us. For even though we knew we'd been bad, still, as we lay in bed, hardly able to sleep, till the faintest glow of morning stained the cold, winter sky, we were sure we could faintly hear that white-bearded, rosy-cheeked, red-costumed Super-Saint's sleighbells ringing in the frosty night as his flying reindeer took him and his bottomless bag of toys onto our roof.

> lying awake Christmas Eve
> the Milky Way flows across
> the dark ceiling

That endless bag with toys for children all over the world was certainly a more marvelous miracle than the loaves and fishes. Though we knew that Christmas was supposed to be about Christ and the redeeming and saving of our souls, our souls inclined towards Santa Claus and the wonderful things of this world that he bestowed upon us. Maybe we went to church once or twice on Christmas Eve, but I don't remember it. Christmas was something that came into our home and made *it* a glowing wonder.

Though all the work to make it so was done by our parents—we helped decorate the tree, and a few times we helped cut it down out in the woods—it seemed as if the universe had somehow brought the tree and all the lights into our living room, just as it would soon send Santa Claus.

Deep down we did know Christmas was an undeserved gift that came from the love of our father and mother, but it and their love seemed to come to us as the sun and the stars, the beginning of each day, and the changes of the seasons.

> Christmas morning
> a new baseball glove
> under the tree

I remember getting out of bed late one night a few nights before Christmas. Going out in the hall, I could see a light still on in the kitchen. Creeping closer I saw my father on his knees painting a new, unfinished bookcase he had set on spread newspapers. I knew it was for me—I was the kid crazy about books. I already had many books, but had never had a bookcase to put them in. I crept back to bed aching with love for my father, and tearful with regret that I'd secretly spied on him and spoiled the surprise he was working in the middle of the night to prepare. By this time—I was nine—I already knew, or suspected, that Santa Claus was really my parents' love and generosity, but I wanted to cling to the childhood myth they had helped create. Almost as much for their sakes as my own.

from the living room
the Christmas tree lights shine out
onto the hall floor

Whatever was lost in growing up, a little glimmer of it still shines for me in the lights and decorations of any Christmas tree on Christmas Eve, even if it is standing in the middle of a crowded airlines terminal, in a hotel lobby, or draped in snow in a small-town square.

on a train
Christmas lights in all the towns
flicker into the past

A Boy's Seasons

The Seasons

p. 5: The comparison between baseball and plum blossoms is more fitting than it might appear to some readers. Baseball has a long history in Japan (since 1872) and is very popular there. Masaoka Shiki (1867-1902), the last great pillar of Japanese haiku, had the traditional Japanese love of spring blossoms, but was also fanatically devoted to the game of baseball. One of Japan's earliest enthusiasts of the "American Pastime," he introduced it to his home town of Matsuyama when he returned there after attending a prep-school in Tokyo. He had played catcher for the school team. As well as playing it, he wrote a number of poems, including nine haiku, about the game and once used a pen name based on the Japanese word for it. In the haiku museum in Matsuyama, there is a photo of him wearing a baseball uniform. Since Japanese haiku poets helped lead me to, among other things, a love for the plum blossom, I feel obliged to make this tip of my baseball cap to it and to them.

p. 9: The Lone Ranger series of adventure novels, written by Fran Striker, were early favorites and still stand out in my mind for their mythical elements: the mask, the silver bullets, the fabulous white stallion, Silver, and the stoic Indian, Tonto. I got a dozen or more of these books as gifts over the years. I also had several volumes about "The X-Bar-X Boys," (two teen-age cowboys) and many of Zane Grey's colorful and exciting tales about the early frontier.

One of my favorite books was *The Saga of Billy the Kid*, by Walter Noble Burns, a writer who painted his scenes with even purpler prose than Grey. I loved the way he put me right there on the dirt street of a sun-baked New Mexico town just as Billy rode by on his dusty black horse. His graphic evocation of the old southwest through personal interviews with old-timers still in the region, his vivid descriptions of the gunfights between warring factions of cattlemen and their cowboys, and his own eyewitness account of the bullet hole left in the stairwell of the Lincoln County courthouse by Billy's six-gun when he escaped the hangman's noose, all instilled in me a wonder of and love for the power of words.

I read Jack London's *The Call of the Wild* and other books about dogs, borrowing many from the library. There were the Albert Payson Terhune novels. I read the ones about collies, including *Lad: A Dog*. And I read *A Dog of Flanders* by Ouida. I bought an illustrated book on how to train retrievers. That was in high school when I had Comet, my golden retriever—and my own sixteen-guage shotgun (with which I never mangaged to bag anything). Books that promised to help me succeed at sports appealed to me—such as books on basketball strategy or baseball skills. I enjoyed travel books about distant lands, especially those about Scotland and Holland. And novels that took me to far away places: *Treasure Island*, *Robinson Crusoe*, and *Hans Brinker and the Silver Skates*. Though I'm not sure now about *Robinson Crusoe*. Daniel Defoe's writing may have been too slow-paced for me. I may have given up and just read it in "Classic Comics," where I also read a number of my class assignments for book reports.

Though as a toddler I had loved the nursery rhymes and Mother Goose verses my mother recited to me, as I got older most poetry seemed too artificial and sissified to me. As I got into my teens anything that was touted as serious and imporant as literature by my teachers was suspect. This included Shakespeare and all the other great poets of the English language. The only exceptions I can recall were certain kinds of inspirational verse that I thought could inspire me to greater effort in seeking athletic perfection. I remember memorizing Rudyard Kipling's "If" (after hearing Charles Laughton recite it in the movies) and enjoying similar verses in an old book I picked up somewhere called *Pack Up Your Troubles*.

That book also appealed to me because it had been compiled for soldiers of World War I and had poems with military themes and subjects. The title came from a song of that time that went "Pack up your troubles in your old kitbag,/ and smile, smile, smile./ While you've a lucifer to light your fag,/ Smile boys that's the style./ etc."

Spring

Dixie Lid Cowboys

p. 25: Some of the material in this haibun originally appeared in a different form in *Argosy* magazine, September, 1974, under the title "Dixie Cups: Stars Under the Big Top." It was published under the name "Ross Yuill," a combination of my mother's maiden name, Yuill, with her mother's.

Summer

p. 29: "The greatest team never to win a World Series" refers to the Boston Red Sox team of the years 1946 through 1949. They won the pennant in 1946, but lost the Series in a hard fought battle with the St. Louis Cardinals. In the bottom of the eighth inning of the seventh game, with the score tied 3-3, a daring dash from first to home by the Cardinals' Enos "Country" Slaughter on what should have been a single to center (scored as a double) by Harry Walker gave the Cardinals the run that won the Series. Slaughter later said that he would not have attempted it if the great Dominic DiMaggio had been playing center field. DiMaggio had left the game with a twisted ankle after hitting a double in the top of the eighth that had brought in the tying run.

The Red Sox almost won the pennant again in 1948, beating out the Yankees at the end of the regular season to finish first in a tie with the Cleveland Indians. But they lost the one-game playoff. In 1949 they went down to the wire with the Yankees in one of the most exciting pennant races in baseball history, only to lose the pennant by one game the last day of the season. Ted Williams was the big star of the Red Sox. A baseball immortal, he was probably the greatest all-round hitter to ever play in the big leagues. He and second baseman Bobby Doerr are in the Hall of Fame. Shortstop Johnny Pesky (who also played third) and Dom DiMaggio are legendary stars to Red Sox fans. Dom, the younger brother of Joltin' Joe, was my favorite player. He wore glasses—so did I.

The Beach

p. 33: The wonderful pier described in this haibun burned down, along with most of the other amusements in Old Orchard Beach, including Noah's Ark, a few years after the period I celebrate. Old

Orchard never recovered and it looks like its old days of glory are gone forever.

Winter

The Radio, Big-Little Books, and The Movies

p. 73: "The one-line captions" in Big-Little Books had "the suggestiveness" of haiku. Here are some samples:

"Big-Little Book One-Line Haiku"

1. With a Quick Leap He Was In the Saddle

2. They Rode Canyon After Canyon

3. "Hullo, Stranger!" He Greeted Tom

4. Smoke Was Curling Up From His Winchester

5. The Two Riders Left the Hidden Draw

6. There Was No Sign of the Posse

7. All at Once He Drew Rein

8. A Ten-Gallon Hat Was Floating Down the Creek

9. A Small Dust Cloud Appeared

Numbers 1, 5, 6, 7, and 8 of the Big-Little Book "Haiku" are from *Buck Jones and the Two-Gun Kid* by Gaylord DuBois, Illustrated by Robert R. Weisman, and Copyright 1937 by Silverbuck, Inc.; the others are from *Tom Mix and the Hoard of Montezuma* by Wilton West, Illustrated by Henry E. Vallely, and Copyright 1937 by Stephen Slesinger, Inc. New York, N.Y.; both books were published by Whitman Publishing Company, Racine, Wis. Vallely, a fine artist, illustrated many Big-Little books.

p. 75: Wild Bill Elliott rode a pinto, perhaps the same one, in a number of his other cowboy movies. But when he did a series in which he played a cowboy named Red Ryder, he had to ride a black horse. For that was what Red Ryder rode in the comic strip where he originated. The horse was named Thunder. Like the Lone Ranger, Red Ryder had an Indian sidekick, a Navaho boy named Little Beaver. He rode a pinto pony named Papoose. Tonto's horse, Scout, was also a pinto. Everyone seems to know The Lone Ranger's white horse was called Silver, but so was the white horse ridden by Buck Jones.

During this period many boys dreamed of getting a Red Ryder air rifle (BB gun) for Christmas. It was often advertised in full-page color ads on the back covers of comic books. I never got one, but I did acquire an old .22 rifle when I was in high school. I only used it for target practice a few times, shooting at tin cans. I then leaned it in a corner of my room and pretended it once belonged to Billy the Kid. It was in poor condition and not safe to shoot.

[A friend recently, 2007, informed me that his nine-year-old granddaughter wants an air-rifle for her next birthday. Just one of many examples (girls' basketball and soccer; female astronauts commanding space stations, etc.) of how girls have changed since the days of the boy in this book.]

Basketball Season

p. 80: The National Guard unit I belonged to was an artillery outfit and the basketball team, for which I played two seasons, was called "Battery A" (or "The Hussars").

The following items appeared in *Foster's Daily Democrat*, Dover, New Hampshire, on Friday, December 9, 1949, and on Wednesday, December 14, 1949, respectively:

DOVER BATTERY DEFEATS
PORTSMOUTH
AS SIVIRIS AND HEUVEL
PACE PACK

By Everett King

Battery A chalked up their first win of the season as they downed the Portsmouth Battery 46-31 in a wild contest at the State Armory [last night]. Portsmouth held a 19-17 halftime edge but fell before an 18-point last period assault by the Hussars of Dover. Dutch Van den Heuvel and Johnny Siviris led the Dover onslaught.

Dutch Van den Heuvel poured in 12 markers in the first period to send the Dover quintet off to a 15-9 first quarter lead. Portsmouth roared back to outscore the Dover five 10-2 in the second period to lead at the half way mark 19-17.

The lead see-sawed back and forth in the third period with Rolly Tuttle tossing in the tieing score with about two minutes of the quarter left. Siviris scored a lay-up to put the Hussars out in front at the period's end. [In the final period] Siviris, Van den Heuvel, and Rolly Tuttle dropped in 15 points for the Battery to pull away from the Portsmouth Battery and go on to win 46-31.

Van den Heuvel with 17 points and Siviris with 15 points led the Dover unit. Stan Snook with 13 points and Bob Tyree with 11 kept the Port City quintet in the game. [Playing for Battery A: Johnny Siviris (rf), Colbroth (rf), Bob Huppe (lf), Victor Girard (lf), Van den Heuvel (c), Bob Abraham (rg), Young (rg), Roland Tuttle (lg), Dick Shea (lg).]

BATTERY A AND KIMBALLS TO PLAY TWIN BILL HERE

. . . To date the Battery has looked hot and cold. They have the material to be a fine ball club. In Dutch Van den Heuvel they have an aggressive center who could probably play for plenty of clubs hereabouts. Dutch couldn't make the [starting] team last year, but steady practice has made the tall boy [6'1"] a good shot, especially with his hook shot, and he can really get the rebounds. . . .

The Paper Route

p. 85: The road was the Old Rochester Road. My route started from its south end where I lived—just off the New Rochester Road. I walked (but usually biked) to its north end where it again joined the new road (actually a highway) by Willand's pond and then I continued back along that to my house with some branching off for customers on roads to the east around the pond. The route was more than two miles long including the side roads by the pond, but I first had to bring the papers from town (Dover), another three or four miles. I stayed in town after school and picked the papers up as they came off the press at the newspaper office. That was supposed to be around four o'clock, but the paper was sometimes late. The newspaper was *Foster's Daily Democrat*, which is still in existence.

p. 85: Jingle, Jangle, Jingle (by Joseph Lilley and Frank Loesser) was a hit tune of the period, about a cowboy whose jingling spurs reminded him of how lucky he was to be "single," because there were so many pretty girls to love. Another of my favorites at that time was a cowboy song called *Don't Fence Me In.*

p. 86: Tom Mix was a cowboy movie-star who died in 1940. During the war there was a popular radio series about him called "The Tom Mix

Ralston Straight Shooters," with an actor playing the part of Tom. By mailing in a dime (or was it a quarter?) and a Ralston cereal boxtop, kids could get a metal Straight Shooter Badge. It had a dial with a rotating pointer in the shape of a tiny six-shooter and could be used to decode secret messages.

p. 87: "Mr. Slate." I've changed the names of those who lived along the route. I was thirteen years old that winter. The house I lived in is gone and a real-estate office now occupies the site. A new highway has been built through the forest that once stretched unbroken for miles behind our house and a large traffic circle is now in front of the property. A small blue spruce that my father planted on our lawn in the '40s is still there. It is now (1994) about forty feet high. [By 2005, the tree, too, was gone.]

A Boy's Fights

The Third Fight

p. 112: The flag with the big "E" flying over the tool and die works represents the Army-Navy "E for Excellence" award. It was given to a company or plant that had manufactured war materials of superior quality and/or had a high production rate, or had contributed to the war effort in some other special way. For further accomplishments the award could be given again, adding a star to the flag each time.

A Boy's Holidays

The Fourth of July

p. 146: "The Spirit of '76" that appears in the parade does not match the original painting. I looked it up after I wrote my description and found that the drummer boy is not the only one with a drum. In the original, the older man in the middle is also playing a drum, not carrying a flag. There is a flag flying above his head but it is being carried by someone behind him. Since I remember it the way I've described it, I've left it that way.

Perhaps the folks in the parade did a variation on the painting and I've actually remembered it correctly. The painting was done for the Independence Day Centennial in 1876 by Archibald M. Willard and has been reproduced and copied countless times.

Thanksgiving

p. 163: I have taken some liberties with my description of the football game in this haibun. It is not an actual game, but represents a composite of games played in blizzards that I remember as a boy. Jennison and Burke were real players who took part in many great plays against Dover High's opponents. During their senior year (they were both in my class of '49), their team went undefeated for the season and won the state championship.

Headed by Mr. Inside (Jennison) and Mr. Outside (Sammy Sarette), the Green Wave of Dover rolled over all eight teams they played in the fall of 1948. In our class yearbook, Armand Ouellette, editor for boys' sports, wrote as follows about the game against Lawrence, Massachusetts:

> The boys then invaded Massachusetts and upset a highly rated Lawrence eleven. Ed Labbe was brilliant in clearing the field for two touchdowns which were shared by Sam Sarette and Dick Jennison. Sammy was outstanding on punting during the day and averaged 48 yards each time. One of his punts sailed 80 yards. The Wave eventually wound up on the long end of a 12-7 score.

All the games were played away from home in 1948 because of repairs being made at Bellamy Park. So the game in the haibun has to take place a year or two earlier. Bourque and Jennison were on the football team from about the time they were freshmen and could have performed as I've imagined. Jennison made All State both his junior and senior years. Highlights of their championship year of '48 included a pass from Jennison to Bourque under the lights at Laconia that resulted in a 14-7 win for Dover High. Bourque ran 30 yards for a touchdown after receiving the pass. And he ran 85 yards to score a touchdown against Spaulding High of Rochester in a game that the Green Wave won 26-6. George Hester, also in my class, was the place-kicker for the championship team of 1948. He had an exceptional season that included his kicking a field-goal to win a hard-fought game against Manchester Central 9-7. The Thanksgiving Day game against Portsmouth that year was a typical end of the season battle. Again from my yearbook:

> Thanksgiving Day, the traditional Dover-Portsmouth game was played in the customary bad weather.
> Outfighting the Green Wave in the first half, the Clippers loomed as a big threat to Dover's great season. At the start of the third period, Sammy Sarette finally broke loose, and with excellent blocking,

returned a punt 72 yards for Dover's first touchdown.

That was all our boys needed to spur them on to victory, and with Tom Conway and Donat Martel tallying once apiece, Dover High completed the season by crushing the Portsmouth Clippers 20-6.

Among the crowd-exciting, boy-igniting members of the cheerleading squad, there were Ruthie, Penny, Nancy, Connie, Dottie, Dot, Polly, and Theani. All of these girls left more broken hearts in their wake than the team left opponents lying on the field – and it left plenty.

An Afterword

With A History of Haibun and Some Tips of the Cap

Aside from "The Paper Route," which is a haiku sequence about a boy delivering newspapers on a winter evening, the works in this book are haibun, a mixed form of haiku and prose. The title work, "A Boy's Seasons," is a series of seventeen haibun about various aspects of a boy's life while growing up in New England during the 1930s and '40s, and how the pursuit of sports tends to make him see the year in terms of baseball, football, and basketball seasons. 'The two other haibun series, "A Boy's Holidays" and "Fights," add to and round out this picture.

I have used senryu as well as haiku in these haibun. Senryu have the same short form as haiku, but where a haiku relates our human nature to the wider nature around us (which includes bricks and airplanes as well as stones and birds), a senryu gives us insight into human nature itself and the relationships between human beings.

The Japanese Haibun Masters

The most famous haibun, Matsuo Bashō's *Oku no Hosomichi (Narrow Road to the North)*, is a travel journal. Considered his masterpiece, it has been translated about half a dozen times into English. It employs a terse, suggestive style. Bashō (1644-1694), Japan's greatest master of haiku and haibun, wrote several travel-journal haibun, but he also wrote haibun on various other subjects and events in his life. At the beginning of his *Oku no Hosomichi*, Bashō remarks that life itself is a journey, so perhaps all writing about one's experiences can be considered part of a travel journal.

Bashō's teaching "Go to the pine tree to learn of the pine" and his many haiku where his "self" becomes one with the object, and so "disappears" into it, have caused many readers to think of him as an objective poet. Yet he wrote many subjective haiku in which the poet himself can be observed: wondering about his neighbor, parting from friends, or just feeling lonely.

In his prose, Bashō is also subjective. He often writes about his own feelings: describing his need to create haiku, his unquenchable desire to be on the road to far places, and the emotion he experiences before scenes of natural beauty and at places of historical or literary significance. He also speaks of being intensely attracted to the spiritual way of life, while continually being drawn to this world by his love of nature and poetry.

Haibun are as varied as haiku. Both take their form and spirit from the poet who writes them, and each poet has their own way of looking at the world and their own style of writing about it. The other three "pillars" of Japanese haiku, Buson, Issa, and Shiki, were uniquely different from Bashō and each other in their approach to both haiku and haibun.

Yosa Buson (1716-1784) wrote haibun as prefaces to his poetry collections. They include memories of his youth and his thoughts and feelings about other poets. In Buson's haiku, the object usually appears without the poet. And often they have been creatively imagined rather than directly experienced. He was a painter as well as a poet and took an aesthetic, artistic approach to his writing, which tends to make his haiku less personal and more objective.

Kobayashi Issa (1762-1826) was very subjective in his haiku and his haibun. In *Ora ga Haru* ("My Spring"), he uses the haibun form to describe his life during the year 1819, starting with the New Year celebration and going through all the seasons. He also writes about earlier events and even presents some of them as if they actually happened that year. The one year comes to represent Issa's whole life.

Dealing mostly with domestic and personal concerns, he writes on such things as an expected holiday gift of rice cakes that never arrives, his troubles as a child when other kids made fun of him for being motherless, and the joys and sorrows he experienced with his little daughter who died after living only a little more than a year.

Sketch from Life

The fourth "pillar" of Japanese haiku, Masaoka Shiki (1867-1902), admired Buson more than any other haiku poet, and he particularly praised him for his objectivity. Shiki wanted to recreate reality so vividly that the reader could almost reach out and touch it. He wrote "sketch from life" *(shasei)* prose essays on such things as his garden, the shadow from his bedside lamp, or the cloud formations crossing the winter sky. Though he called these *"shaseibun"* (sketch from life prose), or *jojibun* (descriptive prose), instead of "haibun" (haiku prose), they developed out of his writing haibun, often contain haiku, and have been classified as haibun by other poets and critics, including Shiki's own disciples.

Yet, Shiki also balanced his objectivity with subjective autobiographical elements, especially in the famous diaries he wrote during his last illness. Haibun may include many varieties of prose styles and subject matters, but in the end they should relate us to nature and the everyday world with the directness of haiku.

Origins in English

In English, Gary Snyder and Jack Kerouac were probably the first to write prose in a haiku style with haiku (though as far as I know they never called the result haibun). Snyder has haiku, or haiku-like notes, in portions of the prose journals he kept when he worked as a fire-lookout in the Cascade Mountains of Washington during the summers of 1952 and 1953. Parts of these journals were published in *Earth House Hold* (1969).

Kerouac in *The Dharma Bums* (1958) tells how he learned about haiku from Snyder in San Francisco in the fall of 1955. In the summer of '56, he went to Washington and got a job as a fire-lookout in the same area where Snyder had worked. In parts of both *The Dharma Bums* and *Desolation Angels* (1965), he writes about his summer alone on Desolation Peak. Though these passages cover the same period, they are quite different in language and details.

In *The Dharma Bums*, the summer on Desolation is covered in about 15 pages, with only one haiku, while in *Desolation Angels* it receives around 70 pages and includes a dozen or so haiku. The greater concision and suggestibility of the former makes it, in my opinion, the finest example of an original haibun written in English. The latter, however, has several outstanding passages. William J. Higginson in *The Haiku*

Handbook favorably compares one of these passages from *Desolation Angels* with the haibun of Bashō, Buson, and Issa.

Higginson goes on to point out that haibun can mingle past and present, and weave a shared history with one's personal life, as Bashō does when he visits a site famous in earlier literature and gives his reactions, or Issa when he writes about observing a traditional holiday. But it is the poet's own immediate experience that gives his writing significance. "Like haiku," says Higginson, "haibun begins in the everyday events of the author's life."

Doctor Sax

Jack Kerouac presents those "everyday events" from his own past in many of his books. *Doctor Sax* (1959) is an unusual "novel" about his life and fantasies as a boy in Lowell, Massachusetts. One "book" within the book, entitled "A Gloomy Bookmovie," is presented in sections called "Scenes" some of which are very much like haibun. Though he doesn't use any haiku, he gets the immediacy of haiku into his prose by, among other things, writing these sections in the first person and the present tense.

Both Kerouac and I were born and grew up in New England, though he started nine years before I did. Lowell is about 50 miles from Dover,

New Hampshire, where I went to high school. Our football team played against Lawrence, Massachusetts, which is next door to Lowell. In *Doctor Sax*, Kerouac writes about many of the things I write about in "A Boy's Seasons": including baseball, marbles, hockey, and cowboys. He has some great passages about cowboys on the covers of western pulp magazines and in the movies. Sitting in a darkened movie theater with a Saturday afternoon audience full of yelling boys, he waits for cowboy stars like Tim McCoy and Tom Mix to "jump" on the screen "under enormous snow white bright blinding sombreros."

Kerouac's love of such things as the "wrinkly tar of this sidewalk," red brick buildings, and the weeds along railroad tracks is the same as the haiku poet's love of the ordinary things of this world. He has long been one of my favorite writers.

San Francisco

In 1957 I learned about San Francisco's literary "renaissance" from the second issue of *The Evergreen Review*. I still remember the cover, with a blue-gray photograph of the city spread across it. The issue was devoted to the work of many of the most important writers associated with the San Francisco "scene." It included Kerouac's great spontaneous-prose piece "October in the Railroad Earth." Early in 1958, I left my job as a cub reporter in Concord, New Hampshire, and crossed the country to learn first hand about the "new prose and poetry." Though I met some of the poets represented in the review, such as Jack Spicer and Robert Duncan, my most important moment was overhearing Gary Snyder talk about short poems and haiku with another poet at a poetry gathering in a poet's house on Telegraph Hill. This was just three years after Kerouac himself had learned about haiku from Snyder when he was in the Bay Area.

This led me to Blyth's four volume *Haiku* (1949-1952). Haiku held the key to a mystery about words I'd been trying to unlock since I first decided to be a writer. These short poems were able to create through the power of suggestion, with more depth and immediacy than I'd ever found before, that miracle of incarnation where words become the things they name or describe (or suggest!). A tangible presence of some simple thing or event that, while remaining only itself, offers us a glimpse of the infinite.

Tips of the Cap

So here with thanks is a tip of my baseball cap to Gary Snyder for helping me to find haiku—and another to Jack Kerouac for his leading the way to a real American haiku. And many thanks and more tips of the hat to R. H. Blyth, for translating Japanese haiku into simple, clear English that not only captures the letter and spirit of the originals, but occasionally surpasses them. And a final flurry of visor-held hat-tipping thanks for his prose commentaries which are often as enlightening as the poems themselves.

After finding haiku in 1958 and realizing it held the essence of what I had been searching for in both prose and poetry, I went back to New England to study the Japanese haiku masters through the works of Blyth, Harold G. Henderson, and Kenneth Yasuda. By the spring of 1959 I was trying to write my own haiku in a small cottage at the edge of the saltmarsh estuary of the Webhannet River in Wells Beach, Maine. That summer I began reading the results at the Cafe Zen in nearby Ogunquit. Those were my first steps on the way of haiku, a long journey which, after thousands of steps and missteps, led me to these pages, which were written during the first half of the last decade of the Twentieth Century.

Cor van den Heuvel
New York City 2010

Cor van den Heuvel is an editor, a translator and a haiku poet. He has published ten books of his own haiku. Past president of the Haiku Society of America, his honors include three Merit Book Awards from the Haiku Society of America, a World Haiku Achievement Award at the World Haiku Festival held in London and Oxford in 2000, and in 2002 The Masaoka Shiki International Haiku Prize for his writing and editing of haiku books. Editor of *Baseball Haiku* and three editions of *The Haiku Anthology*, he has been described in *The Alsop Review* as "an intelligent and unflagging spokesperson for haiku." *A Boy's Seasons* recalls his childhood in Maine and New Hampshire. He lives in New York City with his v

SINGLE
ISLAND
PRESS

ISBN 978-0-9740895-8-4

Portsmouth, NH
USA
www.haikumuse.com